A CRITICAL STUDY OF BAZ LUHRMAN

STRICTLY BALLROOM

THE RED CURTAIN PARTS

NEIL RATTIGAN

2011

First published 2005 by CALLTS Centre for Australian Language, Literature, Theatre and Screen Studies, University of New England.

This edition published 2011 by:
Fastnet Books
227 Donnelly Street
Armidale, New South Wales, Australia, 2350
www.fastnetbooks.net

Illustrations from *Strictly Ballroom* are reproduced by courtesy of M&A Film Corporation.

Rattigan, Neil. 1946 – .
Strictly ballroom: the red curtain parts.

ISBN: 1463590717
ISBN-13: 978-1463590710
1. Luhrmann, Baz. Strictly Ballroom. 2. Strictly Ballroom (Motion picture). 3. Motion pictures. Australian. I. Fastnetbooks. II. Title.
791.4372

ACKNOWLEDGMENTS

I completed the manuscript for this monograph while I was a member of the (now sadly defunct) Centre for Australian Language, Literature, Theatre and Screen Studies (CALLTS) at the University of New England in New South Wales, Australia. I was greatly and consistently encouraged to do so by my valued colleague, Doctor Felicity Plunkett and I am pleased to be able acknowledge her support and to thank her for her enthusiasm (which included speaking on my behalf at the original launch of the book).

I would also like to thank my fellow members of CALLTS who agreed to let *Strictly Ballroom: A film for its time* (as the original publication was called) be the first cab off the rank in what the Centre had (over-optimistically) thought would be an on-going series of publications drawn from the research and writing of its members. The bureaucratic vagaries of contemporary academic management have meant that, sadly, the Centre is no more.

My gratitude is also due to Mr Tristram Miall of M & A Film Corporation and the producer of *Strictly Ballroom* for granting permission for the use of the frame enlargements that illustrate this monograph and for his approval of the book itself.

As is usual in this situation, I need to point out that, except where duly acknowledged, the opinions, analyses and arguments in this book are my own as, of course, are any errors or omissions.

CONTENTS

Watching and Placing *Strictly Ballroom*

I first saw *Strictly Ballroom* in a small cinema (now no longer extant) in Oxford Street, London in January 1993. Beyond the immediate reason of being a loose end that January evening, I was interested in seeing *Strictly Ballroom* because I had been living outside Australia for some four and a half years. Those years coincided with one of the periodic troughs to which the sinusoidal nature of film production in Australia has been prone since its beginnings in the 1890s, and which have been all-too-frequent since the days of the so-called renaissance of the New Australian Cinema in the early 1970s (a 'rebirth' strikingly if prematurely given the sobriquet 'The Last New Wave' by critic and author, David Stratton[1]). This particular trough was occasioned in the main by two events, both economic in basis. The first was a stock market slump that took place on October 1987. I am able to speak quite personally if narrowly about the effect on Australian film production this had, as a screenplay I had co-written had been optioned by a producer in Perth, Western Australia, further developed with the assistance of the then Western Australian Film Council, but was 'lost' when the production company itself was a victim of a convoluted financial 'shakeout' that followed the stock market crash. Although, in Australia as elsewhere, there are many reasons why scripts never make it to production, my personal experience was, I suspect, repeated in various forms throughout Australia in the late 1980s.

This crash more or less coincided with but does not seem to be closely related to the Australian government ending the highly favourable system of tax concessions to investors in film production available since the early 1980s, the so-called '10BA' rules (named after the section of the Taxation Act which encompassed these concessions). No doubt the stock market crash reduced the sources of such funds overall, but the move towards reducing the concessions (to a point where they no longer seemed an attractive reason for investing in films for the sake of investment rather than for the sake of the film) had begun before this. A number of motives have been suggested for the removal of these concessions. One was the loss of revenue to the Commonwealth Treasury which the concessions had supposedly caused in the six or seven years of their implementation, sometimes said to be of the order of fifty million dollars. A paltry sum in the overall Commonwealth budget, it would seem to me, and I find it difficult to imagine that the investors taking advantage of '10BA' would not have found other ways of reducing or avoiding tax in any case, so the figure strikes me as a 'phantom' figure at best. The second major reason is related to the 'outcry' over alleged rorts being perpetrated as a result of increased investment leading to increased and supposedly inflated budgets, whereby some producers, consultants, financial advisors, lawyers and others of this ilk, it was claimed, were taking unduly large fees. While this may have been so, films were being made, so that it is difficult not to see these charges as being strongly motivated by envy and sour grapes. Finally, there was a cultural argument as well to the effect that the strong 'commercial' (i.e., in the Australian context, 'Americanised') emphasis of many of the films made under '10BA' had led to criticism that they were in many instances not particularly 'Australian'. Whatever the reasons, known or hidden, real or imagined, the loss of the tax concessions removed a great deal of the incentive for private investment in films, and the stock market slump probably reduced the number of such potential investors as well.

So, a mere year or two after the phenomenal success of *Crocodile Dundee* (Peter Faiman 1986), which brought large returns to its entirely private investors, this mode of encouraging investment in feature films made in Australia by Australians was dispensed with.[2] (*Crocodile Dundee's* considerable profits may also have helped sour the Commissioner of Taxation's attitudes to these concessions as they had required tax be paid on only a percentage of profit, and most Australian films, then and now, make little profit). This form of government 'subsidy' was replaced by a return to the previously favoured method of direct financial involvement, this time through a newly created Australian Film Finance Corporation (AFFC). While obviously welcome from the points of view of both the film production industry and those of us interested in Australian film from a cultural perspective, the activities of the AFFC took some time to get off the ground, not surprising for government or semi-government organisations. The net result was something of a hiatus in film production in Australia for the end of the 1980s, and a great deal of uncertainty as to what direction Australian cinema should take, in terms of what sort of films and what type of subjects.

To reinsert the personal, I had certainly read enough straws in the wind by late 1987, and had shifted to the back burner my notions of breaking into the Australian film industry through script writing. I left Australia in mid-1988 to study film in the United States, thus creating a further 'obstacle' for myself in keeping abreast with Australian cinema; Australian films, for all that they often look fully or slightly in the direction of American sales, do not penetrate the American market in numbers, and those that did at that time often had limited release on the art house circuit. As was rather predictable, new Australian films, while still reasonably numerous in 1989 (because of productions already planned or under way when the changes were implemented), were rather thinner on the ground in 1990 and 1991 although not as scarce as might have been thought, or as my own lack of exposure to them would have made them seem to me. So, to an expatriate, and especially one living in the USA, opportunities to view new Australian films were spasmodic to say the least: fewer were being made; few were available in cinemas in the USA; few if any received any degree of critical or journalistic attention in the USA. Not very many Australian films made in this period received much attention at home either. A check of films released in 1989, 1990 and 1991 reveals a paucity of titles that had impact at the time or displayed much staying power since,[3] although there were one or two films which, with hindsight, seemed to be providing indicators as to the direction Australian cinema may be headed: e.g. *Death in Brunswick* (John Ruane 1989), or *Proof* (Jocelyn Moorhouse 1990). The only new Australian film which I recall seeing during some three years in Chicago, a city big enough to have art house venues for the non-mainstream, was Jane Campion's odd-ball and atypical (for her) *Sweetie* (1989). Thinking afresh of this film, it is possible to detect some of harbingers of the 'quirky' comedy that would help define the films that in turn revitalised the flagging Australian cinema. It would be *Strictly Ballroom* that pre-eminently would carry to fruition the task of breathing life into the temporarily winded Australian cinema.

It is no exaggeration to say that *Strictly Ballroom* did, almost single-handedly, revitalise Australian film. For not only were the late 1980s and early 1990s economic doldrums for Australian film production, but arguably they were intellectual or critical doldrums as well. Although it was not fully apparent at the time, Australian film in its broadest context was going through a period of considerable change—a change which is sufficiently distinct as to justify a claim that Australian cinema, since 1970, has consisted of several 'new waves' rather than one followed by a consistent period of 'maturity'. Put succinctly: they are 1970-1982 the nationalist period, 1982-1990 the commercial or '10BA' period, and 1991 to the present, the introspective period. A further change in funding decision-making within the AFFC in 2005 may mean another period has just commenced. It is too early to judge just how the sorts of films to be produced under the new regime may differ from previous AFFC-funded films.

During the latter stages of the second period I wrote a book which attempted to come to terms with some of the things that Australian films were about.[4] It was, however, largely inspired by the films of the first decade-and-a-half and their emphasis on dominant perceptions of Australian identity. Perhaps rather arrogantly, I attempted to explain what was intrinsically Australian about one hundred of these films. In the inevitable way of most academic writing and publishing, from inception to availability was an elongated process and the book's eventually publication in 1991 occurred when the second period was well and truly over. It was still too soon to see or even predict with any degree of confidence what direction Australian films might move post-10BA. Before long, however, *Strictly Ballroom* gave very strong indications of what was to become the third 'new wave' of Australian film, a wave that continued to crest throughout the 1990s and into the new century.

My initial viewing of *Strictly Ballroom* came at a time when I had been living in England for about eighteen months (after three years in the USA). *Strictly Ballroom's* reputation had preceded that viewing. It was being written about and talked about quite widely in the popular media and, I think, quite widely advertised as well. Certainly, I 'knew' quite a bit about it in advance of seeing it. Here, after a considerable gap, was an Australian film garnering critical, media and box-office attention. Reviews in Australia and overseas were positive in far greater proportion than negative, and the domestic box-office was enough to make it the fourth highest grossing Australian film (after the two *Crocodile Dundee* films and *The Man from Snowy River* [Simon Wincer 1982]).[5] Even taking into consideration my self-imposed exile, I was hard pressed to think of an Australian film since *Crocodile Dundee* in 1986 which had received any particular attention other than that of specialist film journals. (I should include *Crocodile Dundee II*, but of course its fame was the result of it being the sequel to the first). I was keen to see what all the fuss was about.

Up front, I will happily admit that I enjoyed the film the first time—and have continued to enjoy it every time I have seen it since. An immediate impression I walked away with into the cold London winter night was that *Strictly Ballroom* was something fresh and new in and for the Australian cinema, that it may well represent that delayed clear point from which Australia cinema could be seen to be reviving itself (yet again) and moving in new directions. Of course, it is tempting to impose clear points of departure or moments of change in what are nonetheless ongoing situations. The success and continuing popularity of *Strictly*

*Ballroom dancing: unexpected narrative site for the recovery of
Australian cinema*

Ballroom (especially through video rental and sales, and
television broadcast) may make it seem, in retrospect, that
its aura of 'freshness' was illusory or exaggerated, that it
simply stood out because it was a critical and box-office
success after so many years of the lack of any such. The
production of Australian feature films had not stopped
abruptly with the withdrawal of the tax concessions and
then simply marked time while awaiting the production,
appearance and success of *Strictly Ballroom* to show the way
to the future. It may be more coincidence than inspiration
that saw *Strictly Ballroom* followed up by two films (with
which it is almost inevitably linked since), *Muriel's Wedding*
(P.J. Hogan 1993) and *The Adventures of Priscilla, Queen of the
Desert* (Stephan Elliott 1993); the three giving rise to the idea
that the third new wave would consist, at least initially, of
quirky comedies. My immediate sense of *Strictly Ballroom*'s
importance and its novelty in the Australian cinema context
was coloured by my lack of exposure to films which had
been made in the (lean) two or three years prior to *Strictly*

Ballroom. I have subsequently seen most of these films, and, with the possible exception of *Death in Brunswick* (which did not have the public or critical impact), have not significantly changed my opinion that *Strictly Ballroom* did and does represent a clear nodal point at which the 'new' Australian cinema moved into its third phase. The only film released in the same year as *Strictly Ballroom* that suggests new forces in and new approaches to the Australian cinema is Geoffrey Wright's *Romper Stomper* (1992). This film's confrontational approach and its far-from-pleasant narrative, themes and characters restricts broader acceptance. It is light-years away from the feel-good, fairy-tale structure of *Strictly Ballroom*—although there are aspects of its social interpretation that rather unexpectedly link the two films.

Strictly Ballroom and Musical Conventions

The fairy tale mode of *Strictly Ballroom* is in itself fresh for Australian cinema. I will examine the qualifications of *Strictly Ballroom* as a fairy tale later. For the moment, it is worth noting that few preceding Australian films have ventured into this style of story telling, and those that did were more often than not children's films, in keeping with the way in which since the late nineteenth century, fairy tales in literary fiction have increasingly been taken to be fiction for children (a tendency clearly accelerated by the cinema, especially through the products of the Disney organisation). *Strictly Ballroom* not only utilised some of the fairy tale mode of narrative structure but even used well-known fairy tale formulas such as Cinderella, The Ugly Duckling, Beauty and the Beast and Snow White as inspiration for much of its plot and its themes. Yet, the odd thing is that while *Strictly Ballroom* represented something new for Australian film, it did not represent something new for cinema per se. It remains the case that *Strictly Ballroom* does strike nearly all its spectators (if reviews and other journalistic writing are to serve as an indicator of audience reaction generally) as being (like) a fairy tale, and that without stretching the definition of fairy tale to untenable elasticity, Australian cinema has seldom indicated much interest in this form. The only true fairy tale film, drawing as it does on Celtic folklore, is *Selkie* (Donald Crombie 2000). If pressed, I might include in this limited category *Playing Beatie Bow* (Donald Crombie 1984), *Mad Max Beyond Thunderdome* (George Miller and George Ogilvy 1985) and *Dating the Enemy* (Megan Simpson-Huberman 1996) and, if it is accepted that sentient and/or talking animals are fairy tale tropes, *Paws* (Karl Zwicky 1997), *Napoleon* (Mario Andreacchio 1993) and *The Real MaCaw* (Mario Andreacchio 1998), as well as the two *Babe* films: *Babe* (Chris Noonan 1995) and *Babe: Pig in the City* (George Miller 1998). The Ugly Duckling fairy tale and some other familiar fairy tale conventions inform *Muriel's Wedding* and this film may well warrant analysis along the lines I am applying to *Strictly Ballroom*.

Strictly Ballroom is, then, new for Australian cinema but remarkably 'old-fashioned' at the same time, especially in some apparent points of its derivation. It has been designated, again in rather offhand or journalistic shorthand fashion, as a Musical. Its connection with classic Hollywood Musical is tenuous; it simply does not have the production numbers or sustained performance (song, dance, or song and dance) which would seem to be the most essential characteristic of the Musical, even though it does have, logically given its subject matter, quite a bit of dancing. It does perhaps have some links with the latter-day sub-genre of the Dance film, such as *Footloose* (Herbert Ross 1984, USA), but again this is tenuous. It is not a demonstration of acute perception to note that it does have the formulaic structure of boy meets girl/boy dances with girl/boy loses girl/boy wins girl through dance (repeat as necessary) that is more like the defining structure of Fred Astaire musicals (especially but not inevitably with Ginger Rogers) than of all Musicals in general. It varies this formula at least to the extent that the girl does not have another (unsuitable) life-partner in the wings (as, for example, did the various characters played by Ginger Rogers). In *Strictly Ballroom*, the girl simply waits through two rejections for the boy to come back—which of course he does; this is a feel-good fairy tale after all. *Strictly Ballroom* may not be a Musical by even loose application of the conventions of the genre but it feels like one in a way. All that dancing; but upon examination, there is only one sustained dance 'number' — the rest are snippets within the on-going story.

It is not, however, that there have been no musicals at all in the Australian cinema prior to *Strictly Ballroom*. Admittedly, they have not been a favoured genre but a couple of them are there: *Dimboola* (John Duigan 1979) — although this was adapted from a musical play, its 'insertion' of musical numbers in the cinematic version was uncertain to say the least — *Star Struck* (Gillian Armstrong 1982) with which *Strictly Ballroom* has some quite strong affinities, and *Rebel* (Michael Jenkins 1985).[6]

Star Struck invites comparison with *Strictly Ballroom* at the level of narrative structure. *Star Struck* is also concerned with adolescent rebellion, with its major character attempting to make it in show business by doing her 'own thing', by resisting the restrictions of the institutions of pop music, by breaking the rules and (of course) discovering love in the process. Although made a decade before, it is not fanciful to see *Star Struck* as not simply one of a series of Australian youth/growing-up films but as an early, if overlooked and uncertainly influential, example of the quirky comedies of which *Strictly Ballroom* is often held to be the exemplar and the instigator.

Whether *Strictly Ballroom* is a Musical at all is a question that arises only upon mature reflection. If the film can also be said consciously to use some of the conventions of the genre, it can be said to do so in a rather fast and loose manner. Despite first impressions, it is hardly a Musical at all, but this claim perhaps needs to be substantiated given the frequent assumptions in reviews and journalism that it is. In a way, dismissal of *Strictly Ballroom* as a Musical is relatively easy: it does not contain anything which can be said to be unequivocally a production number—one of those extended moments in a Musical when the narrative pauses in its trajectory and the actors/singers/dancers perform, whether as their designated characters or not. Production numbers, arguably the *raison d'etre* of Musical, are usually extended and frequently involve a shift in the apparent verisimilitude of the story at the level of the mise-en-scène,[7] as with the innumerable Backstage Musicals where the stage performance 'miraculously' opens out to a quintessentially cinematic performance. One sequence which I might, if cornered, accept as a production number—the dance with Fran, Scott, Ya Ya and Rico in Fran's backyard—only qualifies because it is an extended dance, extended that is beyond the demands of the narrative at that point.

A production number in Musical terms— or just realistic story detail?

Whereas there have been numerous mentions, from the serious analysis of David Buchbunder[8] to the quick-bite throwaways of film reviews, of *Strictly Ballroom*'s condition as a genre film—and that genre is usually the Musical—few if any of these make any sustained attempt to justify this classification. Buchbinder goes no further than to assert a narrative similarity to *Easter Parade* (Charles Walters 1948, USA) and to suggest this as a plot-determined subgenre convention:

> The plot line of *Strictly ballroom* [sic], about a star dancer who, abandoned by his partner, chooses an unknown with little dance experience as his new partner and goes on to win acclaim, refers us to at the same time as it borrows from older examples of the genre, such as *Easter Parade*.[9]

There may well be plots which are conventional to the Musical although many of these are overly simple: the formulaic structure of boy meets girl/boy dances with girl/boy loses girl/boy wins girl I mentioned previously, but this is equally applicable in raw terms to many other genres. But, perhaps more than most other genres, the Musical is defined in both the first and the final instance by its formal aspects. That is, it is music (or rather, of course, song and dance) and the particular use of music as performance and spectacle that defines the Musical genre irrespective of the occurrence (or the absence) of formulaic plots. It may not be the case that all Musicals contain song and dance; the majority of them do. Buchbinder's reference to *Easter Parade* cannot be sustained beyond the superficial plot formula on this ground alone: in *Easter Parade*, the main characters (Don Hewes and Hannah Brown) both sing and dance; in *Strictly Ballroom*, nobody sings at all.

Exaggerated mise-en-scène in the ballroom scenes

The initial confused (or perhaps ill-considered) assumption that *Strictly Ballroom* could be understood and discussed as a Musical (even as a contributor to the very small field of Australian Musicals) might be excused or explained not simply by the number of apparent dance sequences (nearly all of which are part of the narrative and not interpolations) but by mise-en-scène of the ballroom dancing sequences. These sequences resemble the heightened mise-en-scène conventionally used in Musicals, even 'realistic' or 'location' Musicals (see, for example, *Paint Your Wagon* [Joshua Logan 1969, USA] or *West Side Story* [Robert Wise 1961, USA]). This heightened mise-en-scène in Musicals is true of both production numbers (rather obviously) and the enveloping story. Whereas in most Musicals—taking as conventional the way in which stage performances often 'break out' into cinematic performances—the mise-en-scène tends to remain stylistically consistent, *Strictly Ballroom* offers four quite distinct styles. Those parts of the narrative which concern the ballroom dancing community (dance competitions, dance studios, the Hastings' home, and so on) are all imaged within heightened or exaggerated mise-en-scène: bright colours in decor and costume, elaborate and obvious make-up on women and men, coloured lighting effects, use of wide-angle close ups, even exaggerated sound.

Other parts are stylistically different. Most notably, Fran's home and community are placed within a naturalistic mise-en-scène: muted tones, more 'friendly' camera angles, 'natural' lighting. Distinct again is the mise-en-scène that accompanies Barry Fife's untruthful account of Doug Hastings' history. This is narrated (and thus visualized) through a hyper-real theatrical mise-en-scène in which all the actions take place as if within a proscenium-arched stage with painted backdrops and artificial props. It remains, however, that while some of these outward appearances may seem to be related to Musical generic conventions, any closer examination of the narrative structure reveals that all dance sequences stay within the confines of classic narrative realism. That is, there are no shifts to another level of representation (another plane of reality) as with traditional Hollywood Musicals. Further, they are not really production numbers no matter how carefully choreographed or photographed they might be.

This manipulation of mise-en-scène, from documentary realism (the *faux* interviews of the opening scenes) through naturalism and heightened cinematic realism to theatrical hyper-realism has no doubt been planned, but it feels as if it was the result of enthusiasm rather than calculation. Even so, a willingness to do so does suggest a creative sensibility not formed by extensive background and training in filmmaking and production. (The biography of Baz Luhrmann confirms this.) *Strictly Ballroom* invites its putative audience to be simultaneously conscious of and entranced by its aesthetics, by its construction, and the 'work' that has gone into it. The same is even more applicable to Luhrmann's next two films, *William Shakespeare's Romeo + Juliet* (1996) and *Moulin Rouge* (2001). This brings it close to Musical territory again, Musicals being routinely concerned to entertain (and impress) with, simultaneously, the ease with which song and (especially) dance are performed and the effort (the art) with which these performances are cinematically reproduced.

Feeling Good and Quirky

Strictly Ballroom is now routinely and inevitably spoken of in the same breath as *Muriel's Wedding* and *The Adventures of Priscilla, Queen of the Desert*, as if all three films combined in some way to recreate or at the very least rejuvenate the flagging Australian cinema in the early 1990s. Perhaps they did, both economically in box-office and overseas sales terms and in terms of some level of textual similarity—the so-called quirky comedy mini-cycle they represent. The three are by no means the same. Each film has its champions, although the grounds for preferring one to the others are usually barely compatible. What they may have in common may be little more than synchronicity, although it is not hard to see some points of comparison. *Strictly Ballroom* and *Muriel's Wedding* as fairy tales; *Strictly Ballroom* and *Priscilla*'s camp/kitsch mise-en-scène; all three have narratives involving the rejection of 'traditional' Australian social authority, and so on. *Strictly Ballroom* was the first. The extent to which its content and, especially, its success inspired the others, or facilitated their being financially supported, is difficult to gauge. In talking about some notion of a 'rebirth' or a 'third new wave' of Australian cinema in the 1990s, being first obviously enhances *Strictly Ballroom*'s status. *Strictly Ballroom* is also more 'important' because for all its apparent frivolous, feel-good fairy tale nature, *Strictly Ballroom* raises far more serious issues about Australian society and culture. (*Muriel* makes some interesting points about feminist issues and *Priscilla* makes some—less clear—points about issues around gay sexuality.)

It has become something of a commonplace to describe *Strictly Ballroom* in one or all of three ways: as a 'feel-good movie', as a 'quirky comedy' and as a 'fairy tale'. Although these terms are often applied, in reviews and other commentaries, they are seldom explored or even defined in relation to *Strictly Ballroom*. In some ways, they are closely related concepts but each also implies something slightly different about the film. These terms by no means exhaust the uncritical categories into which *Strictly Ballroom* is thrust; a packaging of video tapes for sale in the United Kingdom has the film termed a 'romance' and sold as such in a three-film boxed set, along with *Sleepless in Seattle* (Nora Ephron 1995, USA) and *The Way We Were* (Sidney Pollack 1973, USA). It is really rather difficult to see anything but a commercial imperative deciding the sense of these three films as a complementary trio of like films. I will pass over, without being tempted, discussing *Strictly Ballroom* as a romance (let alone a romantic-comedy or 'rom-com' as current shorthand would have it), and give some thought to the other categories.

'Feel-good' is one of those neologisms of popular journalism that serve as an apparent shorthand for a rather lengthier if inchoate concept. It lacks the subtle and not-so-subtle word play of, say, *Variety* headlines but seems to carry a wealth of implications that may be assumed to be understood. But I am not so sure that I do understand it. In the first instance, with rare exceptions, it is hard to imagine that all feature films do not set out to make their intended audiences 'feel good'. It is, I guess, arguable that occasionally some films attempt to make their audiences feel scared—horror films and some science fiction. The pleasure that audiences for these films get from being frightened willingly is not the same as the feel-good factor, apparently. Some films even set out to make their putative audiences think but too much of this, pleasurable as it may be, may get in the way of the film being thought of as a feel-good movie. I suspect that feel-good implies that a film that earns the sobriquet first and foremost deals with simple, even simplistic, moral issues—or may deal with complex moral issues but in an essentially simple way. As a corollary to this, these films do not require their audiences to think deeply about moral or social issues, but rather to feel satisfaction at both the way in which they are offered in a straightforward way and, especially, in the way that they are resolved in keeping with the black-and-white manner of their presentation and to the ultimate happiness of the protagonists and thus the audience. Feel-good films are about the simple things of life (or what can be made to seem the simple things), especially about relationships that are between two desirable individuals whose emotional commitment to each other overcomes all obstacles. *Titanic* (James Cameron, USA, 1998) would be a feel-good movie if only one of the desirable individuals didn't die at the end. (Probably the most desirable one at that.) Yet, seemingly, tens of millions of spectators gained considerable pleasure from that film. Normally, a happy ending and not too much true nastiness on the way to it are essentials of a feel-good movie. Usually it is a greatly over-determined happy ending. It is seen coming from a long way off.

It is not only what it is about but also how it is presented that makes a feel-good movie. Musical are pre-eminently feel-good movies. They have simple narratives of the highly painless travails of heterosexual romance combined with attractive and talented individuals who sing and dance. Music, both within the narrative and external to it, is often a strong contributing factor to making a movie, any movie, a feel-good movie. But in the final analysis, feel-good movies make audience members feel good about things that don't matter but which they think ought to, and about the way these things lead not to complication or misery (obviously) but to, classically, the very way in which fairy tales end: 'and they lived happily ever after'. And what is more, 'they' deserve to live happily ever after in a feel-good movie (that is why *My Best Friend's Wedding* [P.J.Hogan 1997, USA] is not really a feel-good movie: the protagonist does not deserve a happy ending, so she does not get one).

'Feel-good movie'—happy, attractive and in love

To some extent then, to label a film feel-good is to actually slight it; the term is pejorative or a backhanded compliment at best. Perhaps it is not as damning as to label a film a 'soap opera', but it connotes something similar: that the film is trivial, 'unrealistic', even 'dumb' and most probably unimportant. And yet, there is sneaking sense of approval lurking in the term too. After all, what really can be wrong with a film that makes its viewers feel good— about it and about themselves? Is *Strictly Ballroom* a feel-good movie? Well, yes, it is. One would have to be a curmudgeon to come out of a screening of *Strictly Ballroom*, especially for the first time, and not feel good about the experience. Is it trivial and dumb? No, it's not. I think the term feel-good can be accepted in relation to *Strictly Ballroom*, but then it does not say much about the film. It is a reviewer's term rather than an analyst's; even so, it does suggest something about the film that perhaps ought not to be ignored. At the same time, perhaps it should not be used to exaggerate the film nor, more importantly, to dismiss it (or any film so labelled) as undeserving of serious attention.

The notion of *Strictly Ballroom* being a quirky comedy is, on one hand, rather easily accepted—once it has been said, it seems self-evident. On the other hand, it is more difficult to nail down than feel-good, if only because it is by no means clear what a quirky comedy is in any abstract sense. *Strictly Ballroom*, as a quirky comedy, is usually grouped with *Muriel's Wedding* and *The Adventures of Priscilla, Queen of the Desert*. Thus it would seem, by the coincidence of the timing of these films, that there was a moderate 'cycle' of quirky comedies in Australia, brought about not by the success of one such comedy (which would imply quirkiness could be formularised) but by some conscious or unconscious 'need' in either the film-producing fraternity or in audiences. Later films which might be added to the category include: *Secrets* (Michael Pattinson 1992), *The Heartbreak Kid* (Michael Jenkins 1993), *Dating the Enemy* (Megan Simpson-Huberman 1996), *Love and Other Catastrophes* (Emma-Jane Crogan 1996), *The Castle* (Rob Sitch 1997) and *The Dish* (Rob Sitch 2000).[10]

Defining quirkiness by the 'big three' films would seem to rely upon them having in common that they were all made by tyros.(This is also true of *Dating the Enemy*, *Love and other Catastrophes*, and *The Castle*.) Only *Priscilla*'s director, Stephen Elliot, had previously directed a feature film (*Frauds* 1994). But as a large proportion of Australian films are directed by first-time directors—there is (or was at time of writing, there are intimations of a change in this approach) a quite deliberate policy by the Australian Film Finance Corporation to invest in films with first-time directors—this in itself is hardly a sufficient criterion for defining the form, although it may be a necessary one. Yet, the untried status (at the time) of directors such as Baz Luhrmann of *Strictly Ballroom* and P.J. Hogan of *Muriel's Wedding* may account for the raw vitality of these films, an aspect that contributes to both their charm and their 'difference'—and their quirkiness.

In narrative and thematic terms, each of these films is concerned with protagonists who are in rebellion, and in the case of *Strictly* and *Muriel*, with youthful rebellion against older-generation authority. This is less so in *Priscilla*, as only one of the three drag queens could be described as youthful, although there is still a strong sense of rebellion against social norms at the heart of the film. It is true of *The Heartbreak Kid* in a specifically ethnic social context. *Love and Other Catastrophes* is a youth film, and *The Castle* is about rebellion, this time against bureaucracy. And while it may also be said of *Secrets* and the even earlier *The Big Steal* (Nadia Tass 1990), to do so makes the theme too broad. This is, moreover, too vague and too common a theme to be helpful in explaining why these films should be thought of as 'quirky'. The use of the term may simply indicate a journalistic laziness rather than any degree of critical insight. The ease with which it was adopted does however suggest that these three films, beginning with *Strictly Ballroom*, were different in a greater or lesser degree than

Australian films that preceded them. The difference is to do with their subject matters and their individual styles. After the rather staid nationalistic period and the rather eclectic but too-obviously commercial period, the arrival of the third period of the New Australian cinema was heralded by films which seemed to owe little to either, which were fresh, awkward in an engaging rather than irritating way, and dealing with stories and subjects that were new. New to some extent at least. *Strictly Ballroom*, with its core in the unexpected and presumably relatively unknown world of ballroom dancing, explored a narrative location not seen before. *Priscilla* with its trio of gay drag queens in the Australian Outback, certainly offered as central characters, individuals and 'types' not previously seen, although the notion of seeking meaning through connection with the Australian landscape is a hardy perennial of Australian narratives, both cinematic and literary.

Quirky Comedy: innocent protagonists, unusual social setting, inadvertent rebellion

In engaging in this attempt to define quirkiness in relation to these films and to the Australian cinema, I find that it is not possible to point to *Strictly Ballroom* as an absolute starting point. Even a partial definition of quirky comedy will include (1) innocent or naïve protagonists, (2) charming and non-aggressive humour, (3) unusual or unexpected social setting, (4) inadvertent rebellion against social norms and authority, (5) eccentricity of both subject and characters, the latter both in terms of personality and the actions in which they become involved. With these factors in mind, it is possible to extend the presence of the quirky comedy in Australian cinema back to two films by Nadia Tass: *Malcolm* (1986) and *Rikky and Pete* (1988), although the latter has perhaps a violence to much of its comedy that disqualifies it by criterion (2). It may even be possible to go all the way back to *The Adventures of Barry McKenzie* (Bruce Beresford 1972) to locate a prototype for the Australian Quirky Comedy, although McKenzie's origins in a satirical comic strip in the British magazine Private Eye, and thus its own comic book style would seem to separate it from the more 'realistic' style and narratives of these later films. *Death in Brunswick* fits the bill as a quirky comedy pre-*Strictly Ballroom*, although if categorising is important, it is probably more a black comedy and too black to be considered 'innocent' and 'non-aggressive'. *The Heartbreak Kid* is a fairly obvious candidate for inclusion, as are *The Big Steal*, and *Spotswood* (Mark Joffe 1992), and *Secrets* of the same year of release as *Strictly Ballroom*. *Dating the Enemy* and *The Castle* come later.

Dating the Enemy is worthy of being mentioned in the same breath (or paragraph) as *Strictly Ballroom* because of its strong fairy tale or at least fantastic element. It is also a prime example of a feel-good movie. I will return to fairy tale comparisons further along. In view of the fact that there are a few films before *Strictly Ballroom* which deserve, with critical hindsight, to be considered as quirky comedies, it must be assumed that it is through dint of circumstance—distribution, exhibition and marketing, lack of critical appreciation or attention, lack of box office 'appeal' (for whatever reason), lack of audience 'readiness' for the earlier films—that *Strictly Ballroom* came to hailed as the innovator and instigator of this 'new' form for Australian cinema. It does not really matter that *Strictly Ballroom* was not, strictly speaking, the first quirky comedy. In almost any field whatsoever, historically acclaimed 'firsts' are usually never the real first. Eventually a definition must be arrived at of whatever it is that is being credited with being 'created' by the alleged first and subsequent examples. The very act of defining, while granting one instance (one film) the 'privilege' of most completely exemplifying the type, will also reveal earlier examples or part examples. So, it is actually only through attempting to define what might be meant or implied by claiming that *Strictly Ballroom* is a quirky comedy, that I am able to discern earlier as well as later films that fit the pattern. Later films will enhance *Strictly Ballroom*'s status as an originator and innovator. Earlier films do not diminish its reputation; it is the very reputation that alerts me to the possibility of a cycle of quirky comedies, and causes me to search for a context for the cycle and, of course, for *Strictly Ballroom* itself.

Quirkiness in these films then refers to qualities about these films that enable them to be simultaneously 'innocent' and 'eccentric'; quirkiness seems sometimes to be used as a synonym for either or both of these terms. They are innocent in a number of ways, but perhaps most importantly in the way in which the films themselves eschew cynicism, or do not give a sense of an awareness or worldliness which is 'pretending' to be absent for purposes of offering stories and characters that are innocent. They do not patronise their own characters, and this is essential in *Strictly Ballroom* where the kitsch of ballroom dancing and dancers could easily have become the object of camp condescension. (I am not entirely convinced this is not the case in *Priscilla*.) Part of the charm of these films is this subconscious appreciation that the films themselves are not or do not seem to be simply calculatedly commercial creations (even if they are) but seem to have been made with the same mixture of youthful exuberance, naïveté and slight bewilderment that many of the main characters exhibit. In this, I detect the shadow or the echo of the oral storyteller of folk and fairy tales rather than the distancing effect of the omniscient technology-as-narrator of most motion pictures.

Innocence, in the sense of unworldliness, 'goodness', lack of cynicism or corruption, is the hallmark of fairy tale protagonists; fairy tale villains are, of course, just the opposite, and fairy tales inevitably reward the innocent (and punish the evil). More than this, they often seem to be narratives about the retaining of innocence in the face of considerable odds and temptations. *Strictly Ballroom* may quite legitimately be considered a fairy tale, but for more reasons than this.

Cinderella and Her Reluctant Fella

To take one of the most obvious ways in which *Strictly Ballroom* seems to earn its label of fairy tale, it does seem to owe more than a little of its structure to Cinderella, especially that part of its narrative that may be said to be 'Fran's story'. Fran is Cinderella, the put-upon drudge, 'disguised' by her dowdy appearance, who wins the heart of the prince, not in this instance by fitting a shoe properly but by 'fitting' him as the only appropriate dance partner. As such, Fran may be seen to be one of fairy tale's common figures, the 'innocent, persecuted heroine'[11] both in a generic sense and with precise reference to Cinderella. It is relatively easy in this context to place characters in *Strictly Ballroom* as equivalents of characters in Cinderella: Shirley Hastings as the Ugly Stepmother, Liz and Vanessa as the Ugly Step-sisters, and of course Scott as Prince Charming.

Shirley Hastyings: a fairy-tale ugly stepmother

And various, although by no means all, narrative events in *Strictly Ballroom* can be found to have an approximation to events in Cinderella. There are also borrowing from or references to other fairy tales; the 'mirror, mirror, on the wall' aspect of Snow White receives passing reference to Shirley Hastings, whose obsession with Scott may be Oedipal but whose initial attempts to make Fran in her image and then her rejection of her as Scott's partner may be based in belatedly recognising her as a rival. The greater proportion of fairy-tale resemblances and references are to Cinderella specifically, but there is also quite a lot of story material and narrative incident that do not connect with any reasonably well-known version of the Cinderella story. But to pursue these further without better consideration of the defining characteristics of fairy tales in general is to engage the same sort of (apparently) slipshod analysis that led to *Strictly Ballroom* being so easily and seemingly unproblematically called a fairy tale in the first place.

One of the clearest and most defining characteristics of the fairy tale is the place within all fairy-tale narratives of magic or fantasy, the existence of a magic realm into which the protagonists enter or which comes to meet or involve them as a matter of course. The magical or the marvellous is taken for granted in fairy tales—indeed a fairy tale would not exist without magic, at least not as a fairy tale. As Stephen Swann Jones argues, 'fairy tales depict magical or marvellous events or phenomena as a valid part of human existence'[12]. The supernatural is fundamental to fairy tales; this is perhaps self-evident from the very taxonomic category, fairy tale, but it is also seemingly the easiest to overlook. It may well be than when *Strictly Ballroom* is called, in an offhand manner, a fairy tale what is actually meant is 'fairy tale-like', because, prima facie, there does not seem anything of the supernatural or the fantastic in *Strictly Ballroom*'s narrative. Again, Jones would seem to confirm this when he states that 'the function or meaning of the fantasy in fairy tales is related to its generic characteristic of addressing issues of everyday life, of dramatizing the desires and foibles of human nature. One essential characteristic of the fairy tale is that it presents these quotidian concerns in nonmimetic ways'.[13] The essential condition of 'nonmimetic ways' would seem to rule out *Strictly Ballroom* as a fairy tale, but I would like to argue to the contrary.

In order to discuss a film as a fairy tale, one must take account of the essential filmic quality of reproducing (or seeming to reproduce) tangible materiality, the inescapable pull for cinema towards verisimilitude as a consequence of its essential characteristic of photography (even in these times of greater reliance on computer-generated images). There are, of course, films which quite consciously set out to use the technology of cinema to create the fantastic or the nonmimetic. Ignoring animated versions of fairy tales, such as the Disney films, there are many films which deliberately (and paradoxically) use the mimetic tendencies of the cinema to create nonmimetic images—the many live-action versions of well-known fairy tales.[14] In those films which do create the visual and aural appearances of fantasy (or of fantastic phenomena), this is clearly a 'plus' in terms of Jones' definition of the fairy tale. In films which do not, in terms of either overt narrative or mise-en-scène, produce the images of 'fantasy', this is something of a problem in arguing for the depiction of 'quotidian concerns in nonmimetic ways'. But it is still possible to argue that certain films reveal fairy tale-like narrative structures or resemble fairy tales in some other ways than the 'intrusion' of the marvellous and the supernatural. It is also the case that some of the themes (or psychic concerns) of the fairy-tale genre may be present transparently in some films, such as *Strictly Ballroom*, leading to a sense that they are fairy tales—by which is meant they are like fairy tales.

The verisimilitude brought about by cinema's nexus with the (re)production of material reality can be extraordinarily powerful in (re)presenting the appearance of the fantastic, marvellous or magical aspects of fairy tales—or, in some way, of eating its fairy-tale cake and having it by giving a technically-based approximation of oral storytelling (although narrative fiction films are stories being told that have no story teller as such) and visualization of the magic itself, which no storyteller could emulate.

Magic can become 'real' in films in an analogous way to magic being 'real' in fairy tales; there can be a continuity between the seeming verisimilitude of everyday appearance and that of magical appearance simply by both existing within any film's mise-en-scène as a matter of course. This is a characteristic of cinema which can be confirmed by simply citing the example of Musicals in which characters sing and dance as part of their normal behaviour—and I refer to Musicals in which the characters are not, as part of their character, singers or dancers.

Strictly Ballroom reveals this seamless but distinct integration of quotidian and magical within its mise-en-scène. The sequences which are located within the realm of ballroom dancing are those of the magical world, those which take place in and around Fran's home are located within the 'real' everyday world. It is significant that the film's narrative only takes place within these two locations; any sense of a wider actual world (i.e. 1990s Australian urban environment) is nonexistent. There are only a couple of night-time wide shots of the building in which Kendall's Dance Studio is located, which reveal an empty cityscape, and a night-time sequence of Scott and Fran near a power station, together with the unexpected and effective wide shot of Fran's home with a diesel locomotive thundering past, to suggest the existence of a wider social or environmental context for the narrative.

The realm of ballroom dancing is the magical realm of *Strictly Ballroom*. The highly stylised manner of its visualisation confirms this. Here, the colours of its world are brighter, saturated, and artificial. The way in which the people within are dressed and made up creates resonances of the Oz into which Dorothy drops in *The Wizard of Oz* (Victor Fleming 1938, USA). Fran is the Dorothy of *Strictly Ballroom*, and stands out from the others in the same way: she is irrevocably ordinary in appearance from the outset, and surrounded by the equivalent of Munchkins and other magical creatures. As is well-known, in *The Wizard of Oz* the difference between Kansas and Oz, between quotidian reality and magical fantasy is over-determined by one being black-and-white, the other radiant Technicolor—the same distinction reversed for satirical purposes in the later British film *A Matter of Life and Death* (Michael Powell and Emeric Pressburger 1946), where the ordinary world is coloured and Heaven is black-and-white. *Strictly Ballroom*'s distinction between the two realms is less stridently obvious but then the two worlds are, like fairy tales, more continuous. Characters move between the two without the 'aid' of devices such as tornadoes (*The Wizard of Oz*) or comas (*A Matter of Life and Death*). How they get from one to the other is, unlike Dorothy's journey via a tornado, never shown. It is implied at one stage that Scott and Fran walk from one, Kendall's Dance Studio (magical), to the other Fran's home (quotidian). But here, as with the rest of the film, there is no sense of an ongoing 'natural' world of which ballroom dancing or rundown inner city milk bars are but a small part—most of the walk is ellipsed. This aids the interpretation of *Strictly Ballroom* as a fairy tale by ignoring the possibility of the existence of a wider, recognisable social milieu, that ballroom dancing is just something some Australians do. Oz is all there is beyond the rainbow; ballroom dancing is all there is in this magical realm.

Appearance, or reproduction, of a magical realm is clearly important to understanding *Strictly Ballroom* as a fairy tale but it is not sufficient in itself to explain it as a fairy tale. It may be the least important. The narrative itself is modelled upon fairy-tale form. There are, in fact, two fairy tale narratives within *Strictly Ballroom*, or rather there are two ways of looking at *Strictly Ballroom* as a fairy tale, by taking different protagonists as the 'heroes' of the fairy tale. Any straightforward narrative analysis of *Strictly Ballroom* would find that Scott Hastings is the protagonist of the narrative; it is his story. He is the causal agent of most of the actions and incidents, his needs and desires drive the narrative. In terms of this being a fairy tale, how then does it 'work'? With Scott as the hero, the fairy tale in essence is something like this:

Once upon a time there lived a prince, called Scott. He lived in an enchanted realm where all the people engaged in ballroom dancing—a highly stylised competitive dance form designed to see who were true princes and princesses. The realm was ruled by a tyrant, President Barry Fife who had usurped the throne through deceit from Scott's father, Doug, many years before. Scott did not know his father was the rightful king of ballroom dancing. One day, at an important competition, he danced some steps of his own. The realm of Ballroom Dancing was scandalised as it was forbidden to dance any steps except those President Barry Fife said could be danced. Scott, however, was determined to continue to dance his own steps. One night, while practising his own steps, he was seen by Fran, an outsider who was learning to dance but who had to do all sorts of menial tasks in the dance studio. Fran plucked up her courage and told Scott that she liked his steps and that she would like to dance with him. Scott was enraged: he was a prince and she was a commoner and she had no right to ask to dance with him. But when Fran accused him of being afraid, he decided to let her dance with him. Scott and Fran danced together in secret while his parents and friends tried to find Scott a new princess to dance with. On the night when Scott and Fran decided to show the rest of the people that they could dance together, using their own steps, President Barry Fife arranged that Scott should dance with the highest princess of all, Tina Sparkle. Despite Scott's mother sending Fran away, Scott refused to dance with Princess Tina Sparkle. He pursued Fran to her lowly home and there, confronted by Fran's angry father, he and Fran danced for her father and his friends. But her father and his friends all laughed at Scott. This is not the way to dance, they exclaimed, and Fran's father showed Scott the way his people danced. Fran's Grandmother offered to teach Scott. Scott and Fran danced with Fran's father and Fran's grandmother, and they knew they would dance their new dance at the biggest competition of all. President Barry Fife decided he must stop Scott dancing his new steps, and late one night he told Scott a story about Doug and how he could have been the king of ballroom dancing but that Doug too wanted to dance his own steps, and when he did, he lost the competition and never danced again. Rather than hurt his father further, Scott agreed to dance with Princess Liz again, even though he had fallen in love with Fran. On the night of the big competition, Doug learned that President Barry Fife had lied to Scott, and he told Scott that he had never danced at the big competition, and that he and Shirley, Scott's mother, had lived their lives in fear. Scott stopped Fran from leaving, and together they entered the ballroom and began to dance. President Barry Fife tried to stop them, but all the people, led by Doug, started clapping in rhythm and Scott and Fran danced. President Barry Fife was defeated and all the people joined Scott and Fran in a dance to celebrate their newfound freedom.

That the story of *Strictly Ballroom* can be given in such a way as to emphasise its fairy tale-like characteristics does not of itself prove that *Strictly Ballroom* is a fairy tale. To do what I have just done illustrates the difference which narratologists have asserted between story and plot, the former being the essential narrative being 'told' but the latter being the very way the individual narrative unfolds in the precise sequence in which it does so. While it may be tempting and amusing to do so, it is far from the case that any film may be summarised in story terms in such a way as to make it sound like a fairy tale. Any effort to do so with many films would be ludicrous. *Strictly Ballroom* lends itself rather obviously to this; it does not have to be 'forced' into a fairy-tale mode.

With Scott as the protagonist of this fairy-tale narrative, commonalities with other fairy tales and fairy-tale forms can be seen to exist. In keeping with most male-centred fairy tales, the protagonist has a special ability. In this case, this is the ability to dance. As Shirley Hastings (an 'evil' mother in fairy-tale tradition inasmuch as she tries to 'harm' her son by keeping him 'imprisoned') observes, 'Scott won most of the trophies in this room...my son was a champion'.

Scott's special abilities are not simply to be able to dance better than anyone else in the restricted world of Ballroom Dancing, but also to be able to create and dance his own steps. That he is different from all the others is revealed in the way he is dressed, which is always 'simpler' than the others, even when he is actually engaged in ballroom dancing, but also when he is not. In this, he is clearly contrasted with the 'false' champion/prince Ken Railings, who is always dressed in flashy white or silver costumes, on or off the ballroom floor.[15]

Barry Fife: Fairy Tale tyrant and usurper –evil and threatening

Male-centred fairy tales conventionally base their narratives around the hostility of the young male protagonist to an older male authoritarian figure, often one for whom the protagonist has to undertake certain tasks, the consequences of which provide the protagonist with tools or knowledge he can use against the older male. This latter aspect is not present in the sense that the task is designated by the authority figure in *Strictly Ballroom*—the former aspect is. In *Strictly Ballroom*, the hostility is directed downwards from the authority figure, Barry Fife the tyrant and usurper, towards Scott when he threatens the stability of Ballroom Dancing through challenging the rigidity of the laws of the realm.

Even so, it is Scott who manifests hostility more openly for the most part, but Barry Fife's aggression is shown openly in the face-to-face confrontation in the servery. This confrontation only causes Scott to be more determined than ever. Barry Fife later resorts to dissembling to try to achieve his aims—again, quite common in fairy tales. Nonetheless, the structure of *Strictly Ballroom* firmly places Scott in conflict with authority, an authority which is based in older males—ineffectually in Les Kendall (and Shirley Hastings, who 'wears the pants' in the Hasting's family) and most obviously in Barry Fife. Unlike many fairy tales, however, Scott's 'task' is not to reconcile youthful rebellion with existing social authority but to disrupt and destroy that existing social authority to allow a more free community-based authority to replace dictatorship.[16] But the comparison with fairy tales is still valid because, although the film does not go beyond an implied 'and they lived happily ever after', it does indicate that ballroom dancing will continue. Scott's task has not been to bring about a new social order (in which dancing has no part) but to bring about a new social order of dancing.

Interpreters of fairy tales tend to see, understandably, male authority figures who would thwart the young male protagonist, as father figures. One does not have to be a dyed-in-the-wool Freudian or Jungian to see the attraction of this interpretation. Further, these father figures (whether they are literal fathers or not) tend in fairy tales to be of two types: good and ineffectual or evil and threatening. The clear contrast between Scott's biological father, Doug (good and ineffectual) and Barry Fife (evil and threatening) is perhaps painfully obvious. The manner in which Jones describes the conventional relationships of male fairy-tale protagonists to father/authority figures may be applied without modification to the situation in *Strictly Ballroom*:

> At the outset, the young man views his father as essentially good but weak: the peasant is the good side of the father who created the protagonist but is unable to protect him from the bad side of the father, the manipulative king. The king as imposer of laws and authority is an appropriate figure to represent the authoritarian side of the father, the side that the maturing young man inevitably resents. [The role of the good father] in creating and nurturing the protagonist [is] in direct contrast to that of the king, whose chief function is to enforce the laws and impose restrictions upon the protagonist, and whose chief desire is to eliminate this presumptuous rival.[17]

Doug Hastings falls into the category of the weak father, concerned but helpless, and Barry Fife more than fits the role of the king, lawgiver and law enforcer whose intention is to 'eliminate the presumptuous' Scott. The situation is slightly more complicated by Doug being, in fact, the legitimate king, whose throne has been usurped by the unscrupulous Barry.

Scott is unaware of the true nature of his father, even after Barry reveals Doug's history in a carefully blended mixture of truth and lies in order to subdue Scott by appealing to his filial duty. It is, however, the revelation of the truth by Doug including Shirley's dishonourable part in the 'treachery' that cost him his crown which enables Scott's journey to maturity by simultaneously defying Barry Fife and also shifting his allegiance from his evil/corrupt/fearful/misguided mother to his father. Scott's dancing with Fran, and using their own steps, breaks the evil spell that has held Ballroom Dancing in its thrall. The fairy tale concludes, however, without Scott taking the place of the deposed false King, or even an implication that Doug will claim the 'throne'. Scott not only creates freedom from oppression but perhaps democracy as well.[18]

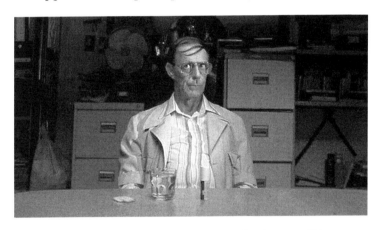

Doug Hastings: Weak father, betrayed husband, usurped king.

There is another way to look at the quest which Scott undertakes, and that is to compare it with the story of the Fisher King from the medieval romance of the Quest for the Holy Grail.[19] This story has many variants—although not as many as Cinderella—but basically involves the hero, Parsifal, healing the Fisher King and restoring the land which has been wasting away in the same manner as the

King. In this tale, the king's sickness is the direct and immediate cause of the blight upon the country. The cause of the illness is far from clear; that is, it varies from version to version. But it is unimportant what causes it; that the king and the community are mutually 'blighted' functions to allow Parsifal to heal both with the one action. Grail scholars have had fun with the genealogy of the Fisher King, specifically his relationship to Parsifal, although it is more or less conceded that he is Parsifal's grandfather. There is no genealogical confusion in *Strictly Ballroom*; Doug is Scott's father. Like the Fisher King, Doug is 'ill'—he can no longer dance, or at least he does no longer dance, save for 'mysterious manic shuffling'[20] when he is alone. Then there is his constant squirting of breath freshener into his mouth—to cover the odour of illness or decay?

The wounded king: disguising the odour of illness

Scott 'heals' both Doug and the ballroom dancing community when he dances his own steps at the Pan Pacific Championship. Doug recovers miraculously, and in appropriate regal costume,—a dinner suit instead of his previous t-shirt and baggy shorts—he dances with Shirley.

Ballroom dancing is freed of the blight, personified by the oppressive regime of Barry Fife, and the entire community are 'free' to dance as they please. Like Parsifal, Scott does not know he has been 'called' to heal his father; in fact, he does not know of or recognize his father's 'illness' until, rather self-destructively, Barry Fife alerts him to it with the intention of preventing Scott performing the very act that will heal Doug. The narrative structure of *Strictly Ballroom* does prepare its audience for the confluence of restoring Doug and freeing the community by the way in it which provides enigmatic scenes of Doug secretly 'dancing' and examining his treasure horde of dancing memorabilia, and crucially in the scene in which Barry Fife 'threatens' Doug with revealing 'the truth' (unstated) to Scott. Doug's enigmatic absent-presence throughout the narrative is preparation for his narrative importance at the climax.

As I noted earlier, unlike so many male-orientated fairy tales, the hero of this version does not accept a challenge, or undertake a quest or task at the behest of the evil king. Scott's quest as such—to dance his own steps, to choose his own partner—is entirely self-motivated. This is related to the fact that the story begins within the magical realm, of which the protagonist is already a part. He does not journey from or leave a realm which is, for purposes of the narrative, an equivalent of the normal world of the putative audience, and then enter by whatever means this magical, enchanted kingdom. His desire to dance his own steps is generated from conditions within the magical realm. Or presumably this is so. The narrative of *Strictly Ballroom* does not actually provide a motivation for Scott beyond his dancing of his own, seemingly spontaneous, steps as a result of an accident, of his becoming 'boxed' or 'blocked in' at the Waratah Championships. Has Scott attempted to dance his own steps previously? Is this what Shirley is referring to when she speaks of 'some silliness in the past'? Beyond this subtle suggestion, the cause of Scott wishing to continue to dance his own steps is, seemingly, the audience's (in the narrative) response to his dancing. This then leads to an explanation for Scott's desires which are grounded in narcissism, and not, for example, in his romance with Fran. I want to return to this, as I think it is a key element in *Strictly Ballroom* as a modern fairy tale, but to do so, I am going to have to re-tell the story with a different protagonist.

Before leaving the matter of the conventional and essential existence of two realms, two worlds within fairy tales between which some characters but especially the protagonist pass freely, it needs to be noted that, even if the protagonist is of the magical world and not the quotidian one (as is the Beast in Beauty and the Beast, if he is considered the protagonist), he does pass from one to the other in a reversal or mirror image of the conventional fairy tale. Scott, moreover, is the only inhabitant of the magical realm who does so—or is capable of doing so. Rico, Fran's father, and Ya Ya, Fran's grandmother, who fill the role of supernatural helpers (even if they are of the normal world), along with Fran herself are able to and do (to a limited extent) move into the magical realm. At least, Rico and Ya Ya do so at the very end when, it might be argued, Scott's actions have opened a pathway for them. Scott must (in fairy-tale terms) make a journey to another realm, which is 'ordinary' to the putative audience but is 'magical' to him inasmuch as it is a world of which he has no knowledge and where things are done differently—especially dancing, as he will discover. He must take this journey because, as a fairy-tale protagonist, he has a quest to fulfil. Whereas in conventional fairy tales, this quest is spelled out in no uncertain terms (no matter how fantastic it might be) by the evil father/king who sends him on it, here Scott discovers the quest for himself. That is, he discovers part of it—the quest for the freedom to express himself, to deny conformity. But there is always another aspect to the fairy-tale quest; there is the literal quest (obtain a magic device, carry out an impossible task, and so on) and there is the figurative or metaphorical quest. No matter what the magical task, the objective of the fairy-tale quest is 'personal happiness' through 'an initiation into a greater awareness of one's own desires and fears'.[21]

It is, however, clearly arguable that fairy tales, at least in their mutated form as mass-mediated fairy tales, literary and filmic, may also offer quests which are metaphorically socially directed as well as personally directed. Folklorists, such as Jones, make a distinction between legendary tales and fairy tales, but film, that most postmodern of cultural forms, mixes and matches to create its own narratives, some of which fall into definable forms (genres) that are sufficiently cinematic as to be seen to exist as cinematic forms in their own right. The fairy tale is not one of these, nor is the legendary tale, but the Western clearly creates a type of cinematic legendary tale and the Musical creates a cinematic fairy tale. Thus, Scott's quest has social ramifications. It is a quest for a way to overcome a social problem: conformity and the stasis that conformity demands. I shall return to this a later section.

I have tried to make a case for *Strictly Ballroom* to be legitimately designated a fairy tale by emphasising those aspects in which it conforms to or has similarities to the structure and the concerns of the male-centred fairy tale. But now I would like to make an argument that confers even greater legitimacy on *Strictly Ballroom* as a fairy tale by pointing out how it is even more like a female-centred fairy tale. Why then did I bother with the case for a male-centred fairy tale? Because in terms of the narrative of *Strictly Ballroom* as a filmic narrative (and not especially concerned with its fairy-tale dimensions), it would seem self-evident that Scott Hastings is the protagonist; it is his 'story'. Under this interpretation, Fran is simply an object of Scott's desire and/or a character who assists the protagonist to achieve his goal. However, to take this view is to diminish inappropriately Fran's role in the narrative; to see *Strictly Ballroom* as a fairy tale does not simply enhances Fran's narrative function but in fact prioritises it. The resemblance to Cinderella often commented upon depends upon Fran being Cinderella, and therefore the protagonist of a major narrative within *Strictly Ballroom*. An alternative way of telling the story of *Strictly Ballroom* might be as follows:

Once upon a time, there was a young woman called Fran. Fran was an outsider in the country where she lived as her parents and her grandmother had come from a land across the sea. Fran wanted to learn to dance in a particular way called ballroom dancing. In order to do so, she entered a magical realm in which all the people were ballroom dancers. Here she was made to do all the menial tasks, like washing the coffee cups and spreading wax on the studio floor. She was also laughed at for being unattractive and was constantly told she needed make-up to help her look like all the other female ballroom dancers. At the studio where she was taught dancing and where she had to do menial tasks, she fell in love with a handsome prince, whose name was Scott. But he was an Open Amateur Champion and she was only a Beginner. Then one night, at an important competition, Scott caused a great scandal by dancing his own steps and not the steps the Ballroom

Dancing Federation demanded everyone dance. This dismayed and angered everyone concerned with ballroom dancing, especially President Barry Fife, who was in charge of all ballroom dancing. Scott remained determined to dance his own steps and late one night, after everyone had left, while practising his own steps he was seen by Fran, who told him that she liked the way he danced and that she would like to be his partner. Although scornful of her lowly status at first, Scott was taken aback when accused of being afraid to dance with her. He agreed to try dancing with Fran and soon they found that they were perfectly suited to each other. Fran and Scott practised in secret while his mother, Shirley and his teacher, Les, went on trying to find Scott a new partner. Although Fran was in love with Scott, he was not in love with her. Yet they danced so well together that Scott decided that at the next ballroom dancing competition, Fran and he would dance together. President Barry Fife, however, was determined to stop Scott from dancing any way except his way, 'strictly ballroom', and he arranged that Scott should become the new partner of Princess Tina Sparkle. Fran was dismayed when she heard this and thought that Scott wanted to dance with Tina Sparkle. But Scott still wanted to dance with Fran. Shirley sent Fran away. Scott refused to dance with Tina Sparkle and pursued Fran to her home. Here, Scott faced Fran's father who was angry that Fran had been out late at night but when Scott and Fran tried to show her father and her grandmother and their friends how they danced together, everyone laughed at them and told them that was not the way to dance at all. Grandmother decided to show Scott how to dance their way. And so Fran and Scott, with Fran's father and grandmother, practised a new way of dancing, and Scott fell in love with Fran. The biggest dance competition of all was approaching and Scott and Fran decided to do their own dance. But President Barry Fife had other ideas and one night he told Scott a story about how Scott's own father,

Doug had been the greatest dancer in all the realm but that he had wanted to dance his own steps. But when Doug did dance his own steps at the most important competition, he lost and never danced again. Scott had not known his father had ever danced and to avoid causing his father more suffering, agreed to dance the way Barry Fife wanted. On the night of the big competition, however, Scott's father told Scott the truth, that he had not danced at the big competition and that Scott's mother had betrayed him by dancing with Les. Scott brought Fran back to the ballroom, and together they went out onto the dance floor and danced their own steps. President Barry Fife was extremely angry and tried to drive Fran and Scott off the floor but just as it seemed they would have to leave, Scott's father and Fran's father and her grandmother began to clap their hands in time. And all the dancers and all the crowd joined in, and Scott and Fran danced on. All the people of Ballroom Dancing flooded onto the floor to join in a huge dance of freedom, and President Barry Fife was beaten.

In this version, *Strictly Ballroom* becomes a female-centred fairy tale. Most such tales postulate a protagonist who is a 'persecuted heroine'—who is a Cinderella or a Snow White. There is more than a passing reference to this in the characterisation of and the actions surrounding Fran. Certainly, her place within Kendall's dance studio as a menial suggests a clear comparison with Cinderella, and Shirley Hastings makes an acceptable Ugly Stepmother with Liz and Vanessa as Ugly Stepsister figures.

Shirley Hastings is not literally Fran's stepmother, of course. My argument is that she functions as one in a fairy-tale sense. But as Marina Warner points out, in French the word for stepmother is the same as that for mother-in-law (*belle-mère*) and in English mother-in-law meant stepmother until the mid-nineteenth century.[22] Shirley is clearly destined to become Fran's mother-in-law (if we accept an 'existence' for the characters beyond the conclusion of the narrative—in the happy-ever-after). 'The mother who persecutes heroines like Cinderella and Snow White may conceal beneath her cruel features another familiar kind of adoptive mother, not the stepmother but the mother-in-law'.[23] In an imagined continuance, Shirley will no longer be an evil stepmother by the time she officially attains the status of mother-in-law. Again, as Warner points out:

> The weddings of fairy tale bring the traditional narratives to a satisfying open ending which allows the possibility of hope; but the story structure masks the fact that many stories picture the conventions of marriage during their telling.[24]

That Fran's major persecutors are women is in keeping well with fairy-tale conventions.

> All over the world, stories which centre on a heroine, on a young woman suffering a prolonged ordeal before vindication and triumph, frequently focus on women as agents of her suffering.[25]

Fran's condition as a persecuted heroine, although not dwelt upon, is emphasised in several scenes. Firstly, once the narrative has settled into story-telling mode, having covered in a mock-documentary flashback fashion the important part of the narrative which outlines the disruption which sets it all in train, Fran is seen to be something of dogsbody around Kendall's Dance Studio, spreading wax for the floor while others practice; she later refers bitterly to the way in which she has been expected or ordered to 'wash the coffee cups'.

Franderella: waxing the floor and bearing the 'bad skin' insults.

She is 'persecuted' at home also. Her father demands angrily to know why she is late after she has been secretly practising with Scott and insists that she be at home the next night for the fiesta. At the fiesta, to which she has returned after having been driven away from the State championships by Shirley—another significant moment of persecution—she sits alone and ignored *à la* Cinderella.

In addition to Shirley's dismissal of Fran as a suitable partner for Scott and the cutting comments from Liz— 'you're a beginner, Fran. What the hell did you think you were doing?'—and Vanessa—'And you're really clumsy'— there are also the repeated slighting references to her complexion. While these may not amount to sleeping in the ashes of the kitchen fire, or seeing her pet magical talking cow eaten by her stepmother (as happens in some versions of Cinderella), or other fairy-tale nastinesses, they are nonetheless equivalent incidents designed to characterise Fran as a persecuted heroine.

Many a fairy-tale heroine represents, through her situation vis-à-vis her mother-in-law (or potential mother-in-law) the conflict felt by the heroine in having to be loyal (or serve at least) the interests of two families, her family of origin and the family into which she has moved. There are clear elements of this in *Strictly Ballroom* in that Fran is not acceptable to the Hastings (or at least not to Shirley, Doug seems ineffectually welcoming), nor is her 'alliance' initially acceptable to her father, Rico. This narrative conflict is more like a fairy tale than directly comparable with Romeo and Juliet inasmuch as neither family is truly cognizant of the other's existence.

The fairy tale feel-good element is heavily implicated in the manner in which Fran, like Cinderella and Snow White and Sleeping Beauty and all her other fairy-tale sisters succeed despite adversity and win the hand (and all the rest) of Prince Charming. Prince Charming in the case of *Strictly Ballroom* is, however, no mere cipher, the winning of whose interest (which is usually an instant obsession) is accomplished by physical beauty and a dazzling costume alone. Here Fran has to be rather more proactive than is usual for fairy-tale heroines, who are often too busy fighting off their persecutors than having time to actually woo Prince Charming. Prince Charming/Scott Hastings is not ready let alone willing and able to simply fall in love with the persecuted heroine once she heaves into view. Of course, Fran does not initially heave into view bedecked in jewels and finery and with her radiant physical beauty no longer hidden beneath dirt or disguise. Fran has a quest to fulfil before that part of the fairy-tale model is achieved.

Heroic fairy-tales protagonists are usually male. It is men (or boys) who are given or called to a quest. The female protagonist ordinarily enters the magical realm as part of her persecution or as a way of escaping from persecution. In Cinderella, the magical realm comes to her in the form of a fairy godmother and all those constantly transmogrifying mice, pumpkins and so on (if one takes the Perrault/Disney versions as exemplars). This is less palpably so in *Strictly Ballroom*. Fran enters the magical realm of her own volition: the reason she is learning ballroom dancing at all is obscure, and can only be surmised as something to do with her status at home, her domineering father and his apparently rigid cultural mores. Again, it may have something to do with Fran's absent (presumably deceased) mother — another fairy-tale convention: 'The absence of the mother from the tale is often declared at the start, without explanation, as if none were required...'[26] Or has Fran seen Scott somewhere and set out on a torturous journey to pursue him? There is nothing I can detect in the narrative of *Strictly Ballroom* to support the latter. That she is taking ballroom dancing lessons is simply a narrative given. Here there are semblances of Cinderella as well. In the Disney/Perrault versions, Cinderella does not pine to go to the ball because she wants to meet the prince, but simply so she can do as the others (her stepsisters and stepmother) are doing, although in 18th century versions, it would be understood that balls were the socially acceptable, indeed, designated occasions for young women of the higher classes to be 'displayed' for the purposes of finding husbands. Fran may be simply endeavouring to emulate her more culturally favoured (i.e., not ethnic) 'sisters', although this does not explain how she has learnt of ballroom dancing. Given, however, that ballroom dancing is all that is ever seen of an alternative cultural milieu to her own, any question of why Fran pursues ballroom dancing (and not something else) introduces extratextual considerations; to assume, in other words, that a 'real' Australia exists but is unseen within the narrative world of *Strictly Ballroom*. But the film is devoid of any such references and barely acknowledges the possibility of a wider social context. Irrespective of how Fran finds herself desiring Scott, it is she who is active in this, and not simply (or even) the object of instant, overwhelming desire of the handsome prince. Unlike the prince in Cinderella, Scott does not pursue Fran from their first meeting; he in fact rejects her sexual interest at that time. When he does literally pursue her, it is after she has fled from 'the ball' (or from the ballroom dancing competition) and he does go to her home, although unlike in Cinderella, he already knows who she is and where she lives; no magic talisman is required to assist with the process of identification. Is he in love with her? It is not clear but then in the *Strictly Ballroom* fairy tale (and in keeping with the metaphorical nature of dance in Musicals), to dance together is the equivalent of marrying in other fairy tales. So when Scott tells Fran, 'I want to dance with you' as an explanation of why he pursued her, it is like saying 'I want to marry you'.

If *Strictly Ballroom* is a version of the Cinderella story, then it is one in which a gender shift has the prince being transformed by magical assistants—Fran's grandmother is Scott's fairy godmother who conjures up the magical helper—Fran's father. There is nothing obviously magical about either Fran's grandmother or her father, at least in the sense that they do not 'appear' to be supernatural. This is in keeping with the manner in which those parts of the narrative located in Fran's home are cinematically more realistic, more natural, than those which take place in the realm of ballroom dancing. There is thus a shift in the fairy-tale model inasmuch as the magical helpers are not part of the magical realm (although it may be possible to argue that Fran's milieu is 'magical' to Scott.) This does not weaken the case for Fran's narrative or the film as whole as a fairy tale, or specifically as a version of Cinderella. It has been pointed out in relation to the essential Cinderella fairy tale that 'the supernatural element plays in [Cinderella] but a subordinate part, for, even without the help of a fairy godmother, the neglected heroine might have been enabled to go to the ball in disguise, and to win the heart of the hero by the beauty of her features and the smallness of her foot'.[27] It is also the case in fairy tales that no matter how fantastic the magical realm and the magical assistants are, they are almost inevitably connected with nature and the natural world, so that the emphasis is on the 'natural' aspect of their supernatural qualities. The mise-en-scène of *Strictly Ballroom* ensures that Rico and Ya Ya, and thus Fran, are associated with nature, and at the same time naturalises their function as supernatural helpers.

Strictly Ballroom emphasises, as do most post-Perrault Cinderellas, the importance of the heroine dancing with the prince, although in *Strictly Ballroom*, the sequence of recognition is reversed: Prince Scott knows Fran before he dances with her—although it is significant that he does not know her name at first. He knows her as the 'serving girl' and does not recognise the potential beautiful princess hidden beneath the dowdy exterior. This is the situation in some variants of the fairy tale, that in the guise of a serving wench, the Cinderella character is unrecognisable. Taking

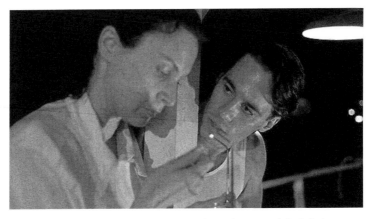

Movie cliché: 'Can you dance without those ... might help.'

its cue from other films this time, *Strictly Ballroom* almost but not quite indulges in the cliché of the girl removing her glasses and, miraculously, revealing her beauty hitherto 'masked' by lens and frames. Again, this does have fairy-tale equivalents, although the items which create the disguise are usually more elaborate (although no more convincing in realistic terms). The point at which Scott does ask Fran to remove her glasses is more a reference to that movie cliché than it is a reference to lesser known Cinderella models. Although the action of Scott asking Fran to remove (or to leave off) her glasses serves the same purpose (removing the disguise, which in many Cinderella stories is more elaborate: ragged clothes or even particular clothes made of animal hides) its effect here is quite muted. Indeed, beyond the fairy tale reference, it is not clear quite why Scott has Fran remove her glasses. He asks, 'Can you dance without those?' and when she nods, he (in the movie cliché fashion) takes her glasses and puts them aside. (It is tempting to be frivolous and suggest Fran must have forgotten she left her glasses on the roof, as she never wears them thereafter.) He then says, 'Might help' before they continue practising dancing.

It is not clear what not wearing glasses 'might help': Her dancing? Her appearance? The development of their relationship? Does this imply that Fran needs to have 'blind faith' in Scott (to use a repeated line from the film: 'where the man leads, the woman must follow') or that she must sublimate her (in)sight to his?

This is part of Fran's process of taking off her disguise (releasing herself from the chrysalis) to reveal the princess beneath the rags but it also signals her willingness to merge her identity with Scott. It is related to the narrative development but in a way that is enigmatic, like the question of how and why Fran comes to be studying ballroom dancing at all. Obviously, in the latter instance, for the purposes of the narrative, she has to be there to provide the catalyst for Scott to persevere with his attempts to dance his own steps. Obviously (according to the cliché summed up in Dorothy Parker's lines; 'Men seldom makes passes/ At girls who wear glasses'), she must remove her glasses to start on the road to greater physical attractiveness. Beyond seeing Ya Ya fit Fran with a new, 'sexy' dress, the other steps in this process are not seen to be taken, just seen to have occurred. Fran gets progressively more attractive as time passes and she and Scott become more involved—another cliché: she blossoms in his love? There is a false step in this direction carried out by Shirley, who makes Fran up as if she were 'one of them'—using the grotesquely exaggerated makeup of the denizens of the magic realm. This short scene, which in narrative cause-and-effect terms seems to have no real point (except as part of a montage sequence of comments on Scott) provides a reference to

Snow White with evil stepmother Shirley addressing the 'mirror on the wall'. Shirley later confuses Fran's improved appearance with her own efforts. But it is apparent later that the Fran-in-love is not a Fran wallowing under inches of Shirley's make-up.

As in a number of versions of Cinderella, the prince is initially offered a number of false 'brides'. The three short sequences of Scott trying out new partners, none of whom 'fit' are the equivalents of the courtiers searching for the unknown Cinderella and being asked to accept the ugly stepsisters, who are quickly found out to be false. There are more serious contenders for the role of Scott's partner: Tina Sparkle, by whom Scott is tempted for a moment, and his erstwhile partner Liz. Tina Sparkle is Fran's most serious 'rival' for Scott. She is introduced as 'the fairy princess of the dance floor', a description made by the floor announcer at the very moment that Fran falsely believes that Scott has chosen to dance with Tina. In keeping with some versions of Cinderella in which a false bride occurs, the prince rejects the false princess. (In some versions, he accepts her!) Here 'Prince' Scott does not need to resort to the common fairy-tale motif of a disguise when he flees from the 'arranged marriage' with Tina Sparkle but it is noteworthy that he is not dressed for the ballroom floor but in the 'informal' attire of open-necked white shirt, no jacket or tie or more elaborate costuming. (He will later wear Fran's father's 'magic' bolero jacket.)

The resemblance to or borrowing from Cinderella are only part of the way in which *Strictly Ballroom* is shaped and structured according to a fairy-tale model. It may well be that because Cinderella is one of (if not the) best known fairy tales, similarities to it are more noticeable. Nonetheless, as I have tried to point out, there are more than a few. Where *Strictly Ballroom* differs from Cinderella but is similar to many other generic fairy tales is in the presence of a quest. Although the notion of quest is usually reserved for male protagonists in folk and fairy tales, in *Strictly Ballroom*, the fairy-tale model is emphasised and not weakened through Fran having a fairy-tale quest of her very own.

Fran's quest is not merely to have the Prince fall in love with and pursue her. In many female-centred fairy tales, the heroine is not even interested in having that happen: Beauty and the Beast and probably Cinderella too. Fran's task is, firstly and most importantly, to deflect the Prince's love from himself to her. Scott is obviously in love with himself. His narcissism, which has more than a tinge of the self-erotic about it, is evidenced most completely at that moment when Fran makes her first attempt to seduce Scott away from his own self-image. This narcissism is conveyed quite literally: Scott is first aware of her presence (her existence even) when he is embracing and almost kissing his own reflection in the mirror. The term narcissism comes, of course, from the Greek myth in which a young man becomes obsessed with his own reflection. In contemporary psychoanalysis it is a named condition 'characterized by an exaggerated sense of self-importance, a tendency to overvalue one's actual accomplishments, and exhibitionistic need for attention and admiration...'.[29] This description fits Scott in the actions and events up to and including this sequence. (His self-absorption is confirmed by the fact that he does not even know Fran's name even though she is a member of what is shown to be only a small group of dance pupils at the studio.)

It is in this sequence too the representation of Scott is at his most sensual/sexual.[29] He has taken off his shirt, displaying his body, and dances with himself, reflected in multiple mirrors, totally self-absorbed and self-obsessed. Instead of the camp, antiseptic asexual images of the kitsch-costumed, heavily made-up ballroom dancers (male and female), Scott is more naturally sexual, devoid of make-up, hair flopping loose rather than gelled into place, his torso partly bare, his clothes simply a singlet and dark trousers. There is something more than a little voyeuristic about this scene, not the least because it is revealed that Fran is indeed watching, unseen, while Scott exhibits himself to himself. The use of mirrors enables Scott to be a voyeur of himself, so to speak, which is a reasonable description of the original Narcissus's obsession with his own reflection in a pool.

Ballroom Narcissus: Scott makes love to his reflection

Fran's quest then is to redirect Scott, the heir apparent to the throne, away from narcissism to where he can outwardly express romantic/sexual desire—and having achieved this, for her to be able to consummate her love for him. Consummation in *Strictly Ballroom*, as in many Musicals, is represented by dance. It is axiomatic (but not universal) in Musicals that desire is expressed through song, and intimacy through dance. But it is also interesting that narcissism is often found on display in Musicals, for all that they are seemingly and transparently about heterosexual coupling. Particular examples of this abound in the solo dance performances of Gene Kelly in almost any of his films but a clear example is where Kelly dances with his reflection-come-to-life in *Cover Girl* (Charles Vidor 1944, USA). It is true of other film dances too: Fred Astaire dances with three special effects 'shadows' of himself in *Swing Time* (George Stevens 1936, USA).

Narcissism defines Scott Hastings from the outset; he dances for himself, certainly not for the poor 'shadow' of his partner who, as Liz says (in mitigation of her involvement in the Waratah Championships 'scandal') 'where the man goes, the lady must follow. I had no choice'. Les Kendall reminds Scott that 'It takes two to tango' and urges him to 'Go to that little girl [Liz] and beg forgiveness, you're nothing without her'. But Scott is unable to subjugate himself sufficiently to decline to dance his own steps in an attempt to placate Liz. It would seem however that his narcissism has been fed by his mother—'my son was a champion'—but without realizing where it would lead.[30] Scott's narcissism is understandable here as Shirley has clearly replaced Doug with Scott; she refers to Doug as 'you stupid man' and 'you silly man'. The Oedipal illusions are obvious, except that Scott seems to have faint regard for his mother either. (Mothers and stepmothers do not fare well in fairy tales, often implying the adage should be, 'the only good mother is a dead mother'.) In the immediate aftermath of the 'débacle' at the Waratah Championships, all Scott can ask of others is 'did you like the way I danced on the weekend?', not how 'we' danced, and when the others do not know or have no opinion, he becomes enraged, a symptom of clinical narcissism.

Scott's resistance to an other-directed desire is signalled when he deliberately rejects Fran's obvious romantic interest in him; his narcissism enables him to recognize and accept as inevitable that Fran has a crush on him but is still too powerful to allow himself to want to accept it or replace his self-love with the love of another. It is only when Fran/Cinderella flees (literally) from the ballroom after falling when surprised dancing with Scott and after being forced back into the guise of unattractive maid-of-all-work (by Shirley/Evil stepmother), that Scott seems to break the bonds of narcissism. But more than this is required of Fran; she must initiate, continue and conclude the process, but from this point on she is going to need the assistance of magical helpers. Certainly, it is during and because of the slow dance behind the curtain—dancing that is both figuratively and literally intimate and not the antiseptic, asexual, faux sexuality of ballroom dancing—that the idea and the ideal of dancing for and by two becomes a possibility for Scott to contemplate, let alone desire.[31] It is this that causes him to pursue Fran in the fairy-tale tradition to her home, where he confronts and is initially rejected by her (apparently possessive) father as an unworthy suitor. Rico is, actually, a magical gatekeeper whom Scott must confront before completing the rest of his journey, both to attain Fran and return to his own world where they can dance their own steps.

Through the intervention of supernatural assistants (Fran's father and grandmother), identified through the mise-en-scène as being closer to nature (as the source of their 'magic'), Scott is able to find the skills, knowledge and indeed courage to return to his world and face the ogre. His narcissism gave him the impetus to want to defy the tyrant Barry Fife but not the ultimate weapons. He needed a compatible and supportive partner. But from Fran's point-of-view, Scott also sheds the last ties of narcissism and is able to accept her love and to proffer his own in return. Paradoxically, it is Scott's narcissism which causes him to want to dance and to be seen to dance his own 'crowd-pleasing' steps, and yet it is his dancing of his own steps which heals his father. He can, however, only dance his own steps when his libido has transferred from obsessive self-love to another, Fran.

Although I am relating this 'second' version of the fairy tale *Strictly Ballroom* as if Fran is the protagonist, this may be the point to say something about sexuality in *Strictly Ballroom*. Fran's sexuality does not seem to be in question; she is sexually interested in Scott from the outset. There can be no real argument that she approaches him (after voyeuristically watching him) because she desires him, not because she sees him as a vehicle or an opportunity to dance her own steps—no matter what she says to him at the time. The narrative offers no motivation or explanation for Fran to want to dance her own steps. Scott's involvement with Fran is because, at first and for quite a while, she is a vehicle through which he can display himself; dancing with oneself in private is all very well but Scott's ego requires that he must display himself in public and that requires an appropriate partner. Ignoring for the moment the possible sexual dimensions of narcissism, it is seems that Scott is asexual. From what little is presented of him, there is no suggestion that he has a sex life—certainly not with Liz. She does, with Ken, the moment she is 'free' of Scott as her dance partner. Scott is also a momma's boy. On the other hand he is a highly desirable sexual 'object'. That is, he is presented as such to the film's putative audience. No-one other than Fran seems to find him sexually desirable, not even the gay Les Kendall, and with the exception of Ya Ya's one moment of teasing when she undoes his shirt and comments 'Bonito cuerpo [Nice body]' no character seems to express or even imply an interest in or awareness of Scott's sexual potential. Yet, Scott is positioned as sexually attractive from early in and throughout the film although at no time more so than at his most self-absorbed moment — the mirror scene. The putative audience is invited to accept Fran as their surrogate, and to be voyeurs of Scott not only in this scene but also throughout the film.

The realm of Ballroom Dancing is devoid of overt sexual activity, indeed few of the inhabitants seem to have either interest or opportunity. Outside of whatever interpretation is made of the 'courtship' of Fran and Scott (and the metaphorical/symbolic meaning of filmic dancing), there are only two moments in which sexual activity might seem to be taking place. One is a quick scene of Ken Railings and Liz in a spa bath together. This is part of the montage of rapid scenes that offer a cross-community commentary on Scott after he has refused to renounce his desire to dance his own steps. (The 'mirror on the wall' scene mentioned previously is part of this same montage sequence.) The second is a scene with Barry Fife and Charm, who is presumably his mistress, in bed together and where Barry is upset by telephone calls regarding the rumours of new steps. He angrily rejects her 'advances', claiming the crisis facing his presidency is more important than sex. (A indication of the impotent state, in regard to ruling the ballroom world, to which he will be reduced by the conclusion.) In fairy-tale terms, this raises a question — why is there no sex in the realm of Ballroom Dancing? Has

Barry Fife taken it all, even if he is not 'using' it? Is, as the heightened sexual appearance of the dancers suggests, ballroom dancing a substitute for sex? Frans' fairy-tale quest is to bring sexual desire back to a world which consists of a grotesque simulation of intimacy (dancing controlled to the finest nuance of physical movement, all spontaneity removed and desire denied) and equally grotesque exaggeration of sexual/physical attraction (excessive make-up, hair immovably sculptured, women's dresses that fetishistically reveal and emphasises their bodies).

If Scott is sexual in the sense that the visualisation of the character is intended to be physically attractive (to the intended audience, i.e., outside the narrative) then in the same way Fran is also asexual or perhaps more accurately, non-sensual. She is meant to be seen as unattractive — initially at least. But Fran's unattractiveness is also noticed by characters within the story, indeed by Fran herself. She is quite deliberately (by the film's maker's doing, not by the character in the story) unattractive in the physical sense as well being clownish or buffoonish. Her first appearance is as an on-camera commentator in the pseudo-documentary which starts the film, where she gives her opinion, 'I thought they should have won', and finishes with a goofy, gap-toothed grin to camera. Her second appearance involves her getting knocked over in rapid succession by Liz and Scott at the Waratah Championships, knocked over again by Liz, spilling wax on the floor that causes Liz to slip, getting hit by a door, and so on. But her motive in approaching Scott is sexual — it is no accident that she is a voyeur of his onanistic dancing in the deserted studio. Paradoxically, Fran represents the intrusion of sex into the sexless world of ballroom dancing. That is, Fran introduces real desire and real intimacy into the realm of ballroom dancing where sex has been replaced with heightened illusion, with the exaggerated superficial appearance of sexual allure that effectively denies its actual expression. Scott's dancing threatens this artificiality and sterility and offers the possibility of unrestricted, instinctual sexual activity; Fran is the catalyst which enables this to occur. Ballroom dancing is the simulation of sexual activity but through the rigorous repression of anything other than its outward appearance, and is carried to fetishistic levels.

Ironically, it is Scott's narcissism which both holds him prisoner in the anti-life realm of ballroom dancing, and the tool which enables him to take the first steps towards escaping from it. His narcissism is such that he cannot bear to sublimate his sense of self to the rigorous, controlled regime of ballroom dancing, but to dance (i.e., to live) only for and by himself is impossible both within the ballroom dancing society and within the quotidian world (represented by Fran and her family). The intensity of his desire for freedom in his own terms must be channelled into a twin desire for freedom (to be different, to be an individual which is one of the social values of the real world beyond the metaphorical world of *Strictly Ballroom*) and a desire for another other than himself (which is what the real world requires as 'normal').

Without wishing to catalogue all the fairy tales (or the familiar ones at least) with which *Strictly Ballroom* may be compared, I have at least one other that seems especially pertinent to mention: Beauty and the Beast. Many fairy tales involve transformations of the Prince, usually physical transformations to or from, or to and from, an animal form (imposed by evil fairies, sometimes but not always as a result of a transgression by the prince). As with Beauty and the Beast, the most common transformation, occurring as the resolution of the narrative, is the transformation from animal appearance to the handsome human form.

Clearly, at the physical level, this does not happen to Scott but through Fran's intervention and her carrying out certain 'tasks' (defying her father, overcoming her fear of being unattractive, dancing in public with Scott), he is transformed from a self-absorbed egotist to a psychologically handsome prince—one fully capable of considering others as well as himself. He first, mistakenly, considers his father then, correctly, considers Fran. It may not be stretching this allusion too far to argue that Scott's original 'ugly' condition has been imposed on him by Shirley and Barry Fife as 'evil' entities. Unlike most versions of Beauty and the Beast (and similar tales), Scott and Fran do not 'subscribe to prescriptions that maintain the power of an elite class and patriarchal rule'[32]—at least not fully. It may be argued that ballroom dancing represents an elite class activity (as distinct from the folksy activities of Fran's community) and that Scott simply exchanges the tyrannical rule of Barry Fife for that of his reinstated father and/or Rico. That the film (and thus the narrative) concludes with Scott and Fran's successful defiance of Fife and his defeat somewhat militates against asserting this interpretation. The fairy-tale conclusion is Scott's transformation and thus the removal of the last impediments to the 'marriage' of Fran and himself. This conclusion to *Strictly Ballroom* does not provide complete closure. Fife is down but is he out?— probably so. But Scott and Fran's relationship has progressed no further than him performing his (or their or her) steps at the Pan Pacific Championships; their relationship has not been obviously consummated in any other way. Doug and Shirley seem to have been reconciled and reunited, and Doug can (or will) dance in public again. But the utopian trajectory (of both fairy tales and Musicals) is only implied not achieved through the community's spontaneous pouring onto the dance floor.

Community celebration of the new social order at the end of the fairy tale.
(Les dances with Ya Ya.)

One of those impediments to the required fairy-tale happy ending in this Beauty and the Beast version, is Scott's 'beastly' state. As I have argued, this beastliness is narcissism or egotism, but another interpretation might argue that Scott's beastliness is homosexuality. Both David Buchbinder and John Champagne have offered ways to address this question.[33] This is not to say that Scott is gay but it is notable that (unlike the Beast), Scott does not seek Fran (or any other woman) other than as a dance partner (and not even that initially), and thus does not engage in any of the stratagems to entrap Fran that the Beast does to Beauty. This initial absence of any sexual interest in Fran can only in passing be inferred to be a result of Fran's unattractiveness (not part of the fairy tale, of course) or to her low ranking in the social hierarchy of ballroom dancing.

Scott's involvement with his first partner Liz seems not to have any dimension beyond the professional. Since there is no evidence beyond this lack of sexual interest in women, that Scott is gay or even latently homosexual (despite more than occasionally conforming to some fashions of gay culture), the explanation appears to be a self-absorption that amounts to an overwhelming self-love.

And what does Fran/Beauty gain from her actions in causing Scott/Beast to change from being a narcissist (or homosexual) to his real self (Prince Charming)? As Zipes puts it, '[Fran's] reward is a move up the social ladder: [Fran like] Beauty comes from [a lower] class and will be symbolically ennobled by marrying the Beast/prince'.[34] Although presented as simple sexual desire, coupled to a lesser extent with a wish for some degree of independence (from a repressive home culture, from the discrimination of the ballroom dancing elite), does Fran really seek autonomy? It seems more likely that she only seeks unity with Scott and not even a unity of equals—Scott will lead in life as he does on the dance floor. Fran has contributed, indeed brought about, Scott's liberation but at the willing refusal of her own. This too is a fairy-tale topos, imposed and reiterated ever since fairy tales became literary properties from the 17th century onwards.

Unlike most fairy tales where the protagonist (or the newly formed couple) returns to and is reintegrated into the social setting from which she or he set out (and was exiled from for the duration of the quest adventure), in *Strictly Ballroom*, the community shifts position, literally coming on to the ballroom floor, invading the previously sacrosanct space available only to the initiated to join Scott and Fran who are the instigators and role models for the new social order. The community signals thereby the abandonment and destruction of the old oppressive social regime.

In this *Strictly Ballroom* apparently denies its adherence to the fairy-tale mode of narrative structure. The manner in which fairy tales reinforce the dominant socio-cultural codes, behaviours, values and social relationships (especially that of patriarchal ideologies) has been often distinguished as a defining characteristic of the form.[35] Taken as an expression of a contemporary socio-cultural condition, *Strictly Ballroom* is inescapably subversive of the dominant Australian social order—or it is if that dominant Australian identity is (or was) that of the traditional Anglo or English-speaking background (ESB) Australian culture. It is possible however to contemplate *Strictly Ballroom* as 'pre-subversive' (or prematurely subversive, perhaps), as reflecting and challenging as yet (in 1992) hidden attempts by certain 'threatened' sectors of Australian society to reimpose the old structure of ESB-Australia, attempts which surfaced in the political arena in the late 1990s, and which were intended (if the rhetoric is to believed) to deny or reverse the changes brought about by the policies and the practice of multiculturalism. I will return to this is a later section. From an analyst's point of view, it is arguable therefore that *Strictly Ballroom* does not resemble the fairy-tale model; it challenges rather than confirms the social and cultural status quo through its conclusion, in which the protagonists successfully confront and in so doing overturn that status quo. Or to argue that *Strictly Ballroom* does resemble the fairy-tale model if the status quo (of the Australia metaphorically alluded to by the narrative) is that of a multicultural society threatened by the reactionary ogre of ESB-Australia.

This second interpretation is tempting in light of the many fairy tales that do have ogres, monsters or tyrants who must be defeated in order to allow the community (society) to live its quotidian existence properly free of oppression and fear. The problem of sustaining this claim is that within the structure of the narrative, there is little sense of a multicultural society/community being the norm which the Ballroom Dancing Federation has suppressed. For the purposes of argument (which I will extend shortly), the Ballroom Dancing Federation and the ballroom dancing community in *Strictly Ballroom* can be understood to stand for Australia; that is, an Australia defined by the ESB-Australian hegemonic national identity. Taking this position, then, it is necessary to register that Australia has been, officially at least, a multicultural society since 1973. Australia was probably multicultural in practice and in the lived experience of a large percentage of its population long before official government recognition of the fact led to both pro-active and reactive policies designed to accommodate the social fact and effects. The hegemony of the dominant ESB-Australia was, in the arena of political policy at least, removed as an ideological practice at that point.

Strictly Ballroom may well be more of a reaction to the image of an essentially monocultural and 'traditional' Australian identity promulgated by Australian films (especially in the 1970-1982 period) and television (especially the ESB emphasis of popular serial dramas such as *Neighbours, Home and Away* and *A Country Practice*) rather than to the actuality of Australian social experience in the late 1980s and early 1990s. In fairy-tale terms, it may be that Scott has to be freed from the inappropriate social (and socio-sexual) situation of the realm of Ballroom Dancing in which he has been imprisoned—although, like most fairy tales, he has not entered this world by some magical means or by a call to a quest adventure or whatever marvellous means but was born into it. That he is not fully of it (or fully comfortable in it) is signalled by Shirley's enigmatic reference to there having been 'some silliness in the past...but we thought he was over it'. The fairy-tale element of a protagonist who enters a magic realm from a situation of 'normality' or everyday reality thus confirms that this is Fran's narrative. It is she who must free the psychologically and physically imprisoned prince, by providing him with the means to achieve his freedom, or by encouraging him to develop his inchoate impulses and desires to escape. This then is a use of fairy-tale mode in which the introduction is deleted; that is, the social setting which is the ideological norm that is disrupted by the incursion of the magical realm is absent or displaced until later in the narrative. In fairy-tale terms, the incursion of the fantastic and the shift of the narrative of *Strictly Ballroom* to a magic realm has already taken place: Scott is already enchanted and held in thrall of the ogre and of the social structure and strictures of the realm of Ballroom Dancing, which is already a magical realm. This is the reason those scenes to do with ballroom dancing are visualized through a mise-en-scène that is exaggerated or hyper-real, that could even be described as 'expressionist'. In this, *Strictly Ballroom* is rather like *Cabaret* (Bob Fosse, 1972, USA) and *Chicago* (Rob Marshall 2002, USA—which was heavily influenced by *Cabaret*) in the way in which the world inside the cabaret club is rendered in a highly expressionistic mise-en-scène (suited to the Weimar Republic period of the narrative setting) while the world outside is visualised in a more naturalistic mise-en-scène. This expressionistic mise-en-scène explains why the 'story' Barry Fife tells of Doug's failure is visualized in an even more surreal/magical mise-en-scène. It is unusual but not unknown for a fairy tale to commence in the magical realm and only introduce the 'real' world as an apparent aberration or alternative realm later. But accepting this, it is possible to confirm the similarity of *Strictly Ballroom*'s narrative to those of fairy tales, and this enables the resolution and the implied social situation that arises from it to be seen as the traditional fairy-tale resolution whereby the protagonist (Fran) 'returns' to the dominant social status quo with her prince, whom she has freed from the two ogres: Barry Fife, and his own narcissism.

To make a case for *Strictly Ballroom* being a fairy tale, even a cinematic fairy tale, in terms of its formal qualities — structure, characters, presence of the magical or marvellous — has also enabled me to articulate (indeed become aware of) some crucial themes. For instance, the importance of Scott's narcissism and the lack of sex and sexuality only really became clear as I contemplated *Strictly Ballroom* as female-centred fairy tale. That it is a female-centred fairy tale seemed at first tritely obvious — the immediate assumption that it is a variant of Cinderella — and only afterwards more subtle and more 'essential' than it first appeared. Given that *Strictly Ballroom*, like all narrative fiction films is more complex, if only by being longer in telling, in narrative substance, than most fairy tales, it is both a male and a female-centred fairy tale in one (as I hope I have argued above). Fairy tales almost inevitably consist of superficial narratives. That is, they tell stories at the level of action and incident, and seldom engage in introspective description or elaborate on character's psychological motives. (At least this is true until the 20th century when novel-length fairy tales develop as a literary sub-genre.) Indeed, most fairy tales provide little beyond that which is absolutely essential in terms of simple description of place. Although it is essentially true that all characters in all fictional narratives are 'functions' of the narrative—they do not exist outside the narrative, they have no 'freedom' of action within the narrative—novels and films, with their distinct (from each other) capacity to create complex psychological characterisation (I am not claiming that all do) differ precisely from fairy tales on this ground alone. Fairy tales do not routinely provide insight into character's motivations, beyond in many cases a simple need for the protagonist to survive or to have a desire to marry the handsome prince or the beautiful princess or maybe just go to a ball, again with no clear sense of why this should be desirable in any individual case—other than the alternatives are considerably less attractive. Fairy tales get to the story points without subtlety; they are less direct when it comes to the themes they are exploring, the social ideologies which 'govern' them at the subtextual level. As a film of over an hour-and-a-half in 'telling', *Strictly Ballroom* has the opportunity to provide motivation, and to make links between character motivation and theme. As I will go on to examine below, it does—to an extent. But it also seems reluctant (or uninterested) to do so. As I have asked before, what motivates Fran to take up ballroom dancing? In not answering this, *Strictly Ballroom* follows the fairy-tale model.

A point to be examined, then, is whether *Strictly Ballroom* is a fairy tale in terms of those things that fairy tales usually do in providing particular meaning, understandings or explanations; their themes rather than their structures and ways of telling. No matter how individual fairy tales are interpreted, there are seemingly some generic ways in which fairy tales function in having social or cultural meaning connected with the time and place of their telling. This is arguably true of all fictional narratives: that they have some connection, direct or indirect, conscious or unconscious, with the time and place, the circumstances of that telling. This is the case with film narratives, and in the critical methodology of genre studies much time and scholarship has been devoted to indicate how individual genres of film provide meanings which are universal across the genre and are also specific to a particular time period, and sometimes also to place (although most film genres are American and thus refer initially to American social or cultural concerns). This is true too of fairy tales. Much of the scholarship of folk and fairy tales has been in collecting and categorising tales from all over the word, such categorising recognising and placing tales into taxonomies that assert their similarity. Thus, Cinderella, by some accounts, may have originated in China some 1,200 years ago and now exists in perhaps a thousand variations of essentially the same story. This would seem to suggest that there are some universal themes that transcend historical time and place (or nearly universal, the Ur-story is not known in some places in the world). But folklorists also, quite rightly, argue that fairy tales have or did have particular meanings for their contemporary audiences in their particular situations and circumstances of those audiences. Thus, although most fairy tales are found to have variants in many parts of the world nonetheless the individual variants reflect, no matter with what refractive distortion, the particular concerns of the culture from which they arise or, more likely, into which they have been adopted (and adapted) and of which they have become part.

Even so, underlying these regional and historical particularities there are commonalities in the individual fairy tales. Fairy tales are, for example, object lessons in social behaviour, and through acting as or providing object lessons in social behaviour, this is what they have in common as a function, even if the specific social behaviours are peculiar to particular historical or geographical locations. So while I have tried to demonstrate the manner in which *Strictly Ballroom* can be seen to be a fairy tale both in its shape and its story structure, I should also demonstrate how *Strictly Ballroom* functions in the manner of a fairy tale, in how it functions as a moral tale, an object lesson, for contemporary Australia. This is, I think, one of its significances, that it is indeed a film which discusses — represents — contemporary Australia, but in so doing it also represents some 'unconscious' aspects of Australia. I have often argued (in other places and in my teaching — I claim no great originality in this) for the notion of a 'cultural unconscious', or, if this sounds too Jungian, then for a 'social subconscious' that finds its voice, its expression, in films. *Strictly Ballroom* does this by touching on something which at the time of its production was not particularly obvious, or at least not something which was on the public agenda in obvious ways; it was in the social subconscious. This was an incipient xenophobia, which was about to become much more obvious and much more openly discussed or demonstrated in the late 1990s, some five or six years after the production of this film. It was to get most attention, having come out in the open, in the political arena, and thus through the news media rather than through the fictional medium of the cinema. It is no coincidence, however, that *Strictly Ballroom* was produced at the same time as *Romper Stomper*, a film which eschewed any allegorical approach to the undercurrents of racism and xenophobia in Australia in favour of a full-on demonstration of it. This notion of *Strictly Ballroom* functioning to provide points of insight or awareness of social or cultural issues is related to the concept of fairy tales as allegories. That fairy tales are allegories does not seem to be a question of debate among folklorists; what they are allegories of is, of course, a matter of endless debate. Having established that *Strictly Ballroom* is a fairy tale, I must now deal with what it, allegorically, is 'about'.

The Importance of Being Ethnic

There are quite a number of ways in which *Strictly Ballroom* might be categorised, a number of taxonomies into which it could be placed. This is true of all films, of course, and is related not only to the complexity of fictional feature films in terms of both narrative and themes, but also because of extra-textual considerations such as the time, place and circumstances of their making as well as the approach and purpose of any discussion or analysis of individual films. I have already discussed *Strictly Ballroom* in a number of possible categories: as a Musical, as a quirky comedy, as a feel-good film and, at length, as a fairy tale. Only a couple of these categories provide ways of placing *Strictly Ballroom* in the specific context of Australian cinema, or in the limited context of the cinema of Baz Luhrmann. As a fairy tale, *Strictly Ballroom* is outside any sensible sub-category of Australian cinema; fairy tales, in any useful definition of the term, are a rarity in Australian cinema and no matter how one stretched the definition, it would be difficult to find more than the merest handful of such films.

Strictly Ballroom, however, does fit well into a category of Australian film which I call, for want of a better description, 'Ethnic films'. To avoid confusion, let me make it clear that I mean by this films that fall, by and large, within the arena of commercial narrative feature films and which are Anglophonic (allowing for occasional dialogue in non-English languages, almost always translated with subtitles). I do not include in this category films that arise from or fall within the rather ill-defined area of 'alternative' film production, although the boundaries between mainstream and alternative film within a fluctuating and fairly unstructured film industry such as Australia's are by no means rigid and exclusive. Moreover, my category is based in films which are about the situation of being ethnic in Australia, about the condition of ethnicity in Australia, rather than films made by individuals or groups who define themselves or are defined by others as being ethnic. As regards this category, it is a matter of content rather than conditions of production which provides the initial defining characteristic of the genre. Such films may or may not be made (written, produced, directed) by individuals who, within the prevailing public perception of multiculturalism in Australia, consider themselves to be ethnic. Some films inevitably will be: a look through the films I include in this genre reveals directors with such 'obvious' ethnic names as Alexis Vellis (*Nirvana Street Murder*, 1991), Sophia Turkiewicz (*Silver City*, 1984), Solrun Hoass (*Aya*, 1991), Ana Kokkinos (*Head On*, 1998) and of course Baz Luhrmann, director of *Strictly Ballroom*. But then there also quite a few 'good' Anglo-Australian names such as Donald Crombie (*Cathy's Child*, 1979), Michael Pattinson (*Moving Out*, 1983 and *Street Hero*, 1984), Michael Jenkins (*The Heartbreak Kid*, 1993), Kate Woods (*Looking for Alibrandi*, 2000) and Steve Jacobs (*La Spagnola*, 2001). Names do not an ethnic make nor deny it, of course. The possession of a non-English or non-Celtic (Irish, Scots) sounding name may disguise an Australian of many generations or a thoroughly English-seeming name may 'disguise' a more recent ethnic individual, as in the case of Paul Cox, originally from the Netherlands.

A bit of background is required to locate *Strictly Ballroom* as an Ethnic film within the broader context of Australian cinema, and so within my category of Ethnic films. It needs to be recognised that of the over 900 feature films produced in Australia since the 1970s—'on-shore' productions that is—it is only relatively recently that many have placed any emphasis on ethnicity or multiculturalism, and even then the number is quite small, perhaps no more than forty. That is, there are only a handful of films which find their drama, their narrative locations and their characters within the condition, situation and histories of immigrants in Australia. For the first decade and a half of the new Australian cinema, there seemed to be very little possibility, or perhaps very little opportunity, of exploring or representing ethnic diversity in Australia through feature films. Feature film production was swamped by the torrent of representations of the singular, monocultural Anglo-Australian national identity. The classic Australian films of the 1970s —*Sunday Too Far Away* (Ken Hannam 1975), *Picnic at Hanging Rock* (Peter Weir 1975), *My Brilliant Career* (Gillian Armstrong 1979) and so on up to and including, especially *Gallipoli* (Peter Weir 1981)—are representations par excellence of the dominant Australian identity. Many in fact rehearse the very mythical conditions which, it was so often claimed, created the Australian character: the bush environment, Anglo-Celtic origins, mateship in and out of adversity, particular history, and so on. *Gallipoli* does so in a manner which can only be called brazen-faced. Yet the coincidence of these films of the mid- and late-1970s and the public and political declaration of Australian as a multicultural society (with concomitant political policies designed to address social matters arising from this multicultural condition) should not be overlooked. It is true that to a large extent these films were celebrations, not simply of the dominant Australian character, but also of the ability to celebrate Australian character, Australia itself in and through Australian films and (hopefully) on Australian and overseas cinema screens. There is a clear sense in many of the films of the first ten years or so of the sheer pleasure of being able to speak 'of ourselves, to ourselves' after so many decades without the wherewithal or official encouragement (often actually official discouragement).

In retrospect it is possible to see the films of this revitalised Australian cinema as not simply celebrations of a freedom to represent 'ourselves'. The facts of a multicultural and not a monocultural Australia, available to many (but by no means all) Anglo-Australians, especially those living in the inner cities and in particular areas in the ever-sprawling suburbs, are so resolutely ignored in the 'nationalistic' films of the New Australian cinema that it is possible to see this as 'deliberate'. I don't mean the ignoring of multicultural Australia, of ethnic-Australians, was necessarily conscious or purposeful, done with intent — although it may have been. But these films do take on aspects of being designed to 'educate' Australians, those audiences who have grown up without representations of themselves on their screens, in what it means to be Australian. At the same time, those films which had an eye on overseas distribution were quite clearly also concerned, with what degree of consciousness is hard to fully determine, with telling the rest of the world what it means to be Australian. The message in any case was the same: what it means to be Australian is to be Anglo-Australian, to be 'traditional' Australian. Oddly then these films may in fact have been recognition of the discernible existence, the intransigent existence, of subgroups or subcultures within the Australian social context. These would be groups who had not, so to speak, taken in Australian-ness with their mother's milk. The educational aspect could apply equally to those more recent arrivals who might 'need' lessons in the 'true' Australian way of life—a lingering echo of the historical official policy of assimilation. The so-called AFC-genre[36] films may have been a conscious celebration of dominant Australian-ness and an unconscious reaction to a perceived threat to that very dominant image.

I have mentioned earlier the three periods of New Australian cinema. Films which I designate as Ethnic films are found in the second and third periods (with rare exceptions in the first such as *Kostas* [1979]), and more prevalently in the later stages of the second and now in the most recent. The 1990s return to government sponsorship for the Australian film-producing industry, even as 'hands-off' sponsorship through the Australian Film Finance Corporation saw (and may have been in some way responsible for) an initial return to films which are more 'Australian', in the sense of not being obviously or stridently interested in ethnicity or multiculturalism, nor, at the same time, in 'internationalism' in the never-ending quest for commercial success. Of the three films so often grouped on these pages as elsewhere, *Strictly Ballroom*, *Muriel's Wedding*, and *The Adventures of Priscilla*, only *Strictly Ballroom* raises any questions of ethnicity, but does so crucially, as I will argue.[37] Multiculturalism, as a social practice, emphasises difference; it not merely recognises ethnicity as a basis of definition, it actually insists on the application of that definition. When it comes to fictional narratives the manner in which films routinely create characterisation through a small number of traits or signs means that ethnicity is often under-explained, and this can have an effect on the meaning and interpretation of characters and actions, even if unintended.

Ethnic identification (although not necessarily ethnic identity) is often made on the basis of physical appearance (which is then linked with or co-exists with such things as names and certain behaviours or attitudes). Phenotyping provides much of the actual and fictional recognition of ethnicity, and characterising by physical appearance is universal in the Ethnic films. How easily Ya Ya, Rico and their friends are represented and presumably recognised as ethnic in *Strictly Ballroom*; as soon as they appear, they scream ethnicity in a way in which interestingly Fran, to that point, has not. The mise-en-scène of Ethnic films carries this notion of an ethnic type of appearance into the inanimate. Architecture, decor and dress are other important signs of ethnicity used routinely in these films and thereby reproduce stereotyped perceptions drawn from Australian 'actuality' as well as the prejudices of Anglo-Australian culture. These types of 'ethnic indicators' are present in *Strictly Ballroom*, albeit in subtle ways for the most part. The most obvious is Rico's flamenco/bolero/toreador jacket, which will also become an important symbol of the way in which ethnicity and Anglo-Australicity intermingle at the conclusion of the film when Scott wears the jacket as he dances with Fran in defiance of the Australian Dance Federation. The mise-en-scène of Fran's home serves other purposes in *Strictly Ballroom* than just to indicate ethnicity. It is ethnic-looking at the same time as it looks much more natural than the ballrooms, dance studios, and even Scott's home. The emphasis here is on it being vibrant, wholesome and vital as opposed to the artificiality and restriction of ballroom dancing. It is, in fact, less alien and alienating than is the realm of ballroom dancing.

This last is interesting because the defining characteristic of the Ethnic films is difference. All such films, perhaps rather self-evidently, are based to some degree in a simple dichotomy (or opposition) between a supposed Australian-ness and a supposed ethnic-ness. These films locate ethnicity through the narrative structuring device of difference. Put simply, to be ethnic in these films is to be different. To create a sense, a perception, of difference it is necessary to have a 'normality' against which difference may be registered and measured. Further, it is necessary to assume the putative audience brings a sense of that normality to the experience of the film.

Strictly Ballroom is particularly instructive in the way ethnicity is constructed and represented within its narrative for it emphasises something which is often no more than implied or is unconsciously 'present through absence' in other Ethnic films. Let me explain this seeming semantic contradiction. This sense of difference—the source of much dramatic incident and characterisation—is often based on an absence, or upon that which is not fully articulated within most of the films: an assumption about what constitutes 'normal' Australian culture. Many Ethnic films of the recent Australian cinema do not do more than hint at that typicality of Australian culture against which the cultural conditions, characteristics, and actions of ethnic protagonists are depicted as being different, alien or 'other'. Australian culture is a taken-for-granted background against which the ethnicity of the Non English Speaking Background (NESB) characters is displayed, and which throws them into relief. That many of these Ethnic films are comedies shows how dependant they are on an unspoken normality (understood and perhaps shared by the putative audience) against which difference can be a source of humour.

I do not wish to seem to be playing some sort of semantic word game when I assert that *Strictly Ballroom* both follows this convention of absent-presence and does not. On one hand, that the narrative of *Strictly Ballroom* is played out within two isolated locations (ballroom dancing studios and halls, and Fran's home, with practically no sense of a wider social or environmental context) makes any realistic sense of a somewhere in Australia that this is taking place into an absence; both ballroom dancing and Fran's home seem equally 'abnormal' (or equally 'normal', depending on whether one looks at it from a social or a storytelling point of view). On the other hand, *Strictly Ballroom* does not take Anglo-Australian culture for granted; it draws attention to it quite purposefully by setting up Australian culture as the opposing culture. This is done through metaphor: the world of ballroom dancing equals the 'world' of Anglo-Australian culture. Through the way in which ballroom dancing functions, how it is 'run', what it gives to and takes from it adherents, its group norms and values, Anglo-Australian culture, by process of metaphor, is shown failing to be a satisfactory culture. This is especially so through the way in which it refuses to provide or permit space for its ESB protagonist, Scott Hastings, to exercise freedom of choice and give full expression to his personality and talents. It does not allow him to 'grow'; in fact, it especially prohibits this in the name of conformity. Further, it is a culture based on fear and repression.

The ways in which the bureaucrats and others within the ballroom dance culture are characterised are important here. First, they are visualised as a carnival of grotesques, over-dressed, be-wigged and heavily made up (both women and men), often shot in wide-angle distorting close-up. This highly stylised visual representation continues beyond characterisation of people to be true of the cinematic presentation of places associated with ballroom dancing/Anglo-Australian culture. Second, many of these same figures, especially ones with authority are all old, traditional, hidebound, uncompromising and often ruthless in their demands that the tenets of ballroom dancing (of traditional singular Anglo-Australia) be adhered to by the members of its culture, without the right of argument or objection: dance this way or don't dance at all. That is, live in Australia Anglo-Australia's way or don't live here at all. This was the basic guiding principle of pre-multicultural Australia: assimilation not integration.

While most but not all Ethnic films do find ethnicity attractive in some degree, or at least provide the opportunity to empathise or sympathise with ethnic characters, *Strictly Ballroom* makes a clear, unmistakable statement that difference in the form of ethnicity is desirable because it is different. This not simply a dramatic imperative, that the difference enables the attractive protagonists to break out and away as the narrative development and resolution requires them to do. The sense of change, of freedom, of difference, of rebellion even, is also taken up in the wider community as the applauding multitude reveals at the conclusion when all—barring Barry Fife, the defeated representative of outmoded irrelevant, traditional culture—cheer on Scott and Fran, the personification of the mixing of the old and the new. They are the exemplars of multiculturalism in practice, which they demonstrate in their attachment to each other and through their new, cross-cultural dancing style. In *Strictly Ballroom*, unlike many other Ethnic films, there is no ambiguity about the rejection of the notion of assimilation, nor about whether integration is workable in practice. If anything, Scott is assimilated into the ethnic culture of

Fran's family; *Strictly Ballroom* may be making a case for 'reverse assimilation'.

In keeping with the approach of most Ethnic films, *Strictly Ballroom* manifests its representation of ethnicity through a narrative centred in the drama of a personal relationship. Although a number of such films concentrate upon relationships within the family, which is represented as a special site of ethnicity, *Strictly Ballroom* follows the 'Romeo and Juliet' formula a number of Ethnic films use — for example *The Heartbreak Kid* or *Death in Brunswick*. (To which, of course, Luhrmann was to turn literally and literatively in his next film, *William Shakespeare's Romeo + Juliet*.) As with those films, one protagonist, Scott, is a representative of Anglo-Australian culture, the other, Fran, of ethnic culture, thus quite simply (in the Australian context) introducing and delineating the gulf between them which their love must transcend, and placing each within a family or community context which would seem to be opposed to the breaking of any such barriers. These narratives then set Anglo-Australian culture against the ethnicity of the chosen migrant culture (although often ethnicity takes on generic form: all ethnicity is interchangeable — to use the colloquial term, a wog is a wog is a wog). In its function as an allegory *Strictly Ballroom* is exceptional amongst Ethnic films in that it does challenge the notion of the social cohesiveness of the real or mythical singular Anglo-Australian culture, and it does so by postulating the greater attractiveness of ethnic culture as well as the oppressive conformity of Anglo-Australian culture.

Fran's ethnicity is simultaneously clear and confused. That is, it only becomes apparent that she is ethnic once Scott escorts her home. For an Australian audience, for her

Reverse assimilation: the ethnicising of Scott (and Fran).

family to operate a milk bar in a rundown part of town would almost immediately suggest ethnicity. (This same stereotyped image is used for a family in *Moving Out*.) This is rapidly confirmed by Fran's father shouting at her in a foreign language (translated in subtitles but, presumably, Spanish[38]), questioning where she has been and ordering her to stay home tomorrow for 'the fiesta'. Strict patriarchal families are a clear sign of ethnicity in Australian cinema (for example, *The Heartbreak Kid*, *Moving Out*, *Death in Brunswick*); and Scott's family is a matriarchal one (although this is not necessarily a sign of Anglo-Australianness but a further contrast for dramatic purposes). Before this, Fran's ethnicity is not strongly indicated by her appearance. She is unprepossessing certainly, plain, dowdy, gap-toothed, bespectacled and befreckled, and frizzy-haired, but not especially ethnic looking in any stereotyped way. If anything, she becomes more ethnic in appearance as time goes on, especially at the end when she is dressed in a manner which is not the stylised kitsch-ethnicity of ballroom dancers dressed for a Latin American dance but as if she were, indeed, a Spanish flamenco dancer. Her complexion is clearer, her glasses (as noted earlier) long gone, her hair controlled, tied back. The film discovers her ethnicity while confirming and celebrating it. Her grandmother and her father are more simply visually ethnic; phenotyping is put to work here. That they speak Spanish (or do not speak English, at least) confirms the information provided by how they look.

The use of phenotyping as indication of ethnicity is, however, a site of some ambiguity in *Strictly Ballroom*. Whereas Fran is at first not especially ethnic-looking, but becomes more so, Scott, although the seeming epitome of the Anglo-Australian world of ballroom dancing, looks more ethnic than Fran. Dark and Latinate, the resemblance to Rudolph Valentino, the great Latin icon of silent American cinema, can hardly be entirely coincidental. It is particularly noticeable in much of the publicity material for the film in which Scott, dressed in a toreador jacket, straight jet-black hair flopping across his sweat-spangled brow, stares straight into the eyes of the spectator, the lighting emphasising his cheekbones and his full, sensual lips. It also seems to me that the negative is deliberately printed in reverse; Scott's hair is parted on the left, throughout the film it is parted on the right. The precise effect of this reversal is hard to define; it somehow makes him more macho and more saturninely ethnic. Given the importance I gave to the mirror-image scene in offering Scott's narcissism as an important aspect of the narrative, this image is in itself a 'mirror image'. Within the film itself, of course, Scott also has these ethnic aspects to his appearance, they are not simply the work of the film's publicist. He also stands out from the other ballroom dancers precisely because of these factors in his appearance, certainly in contrast to the uniformly silver from head to foot Ken Railings, but also from Wayne, who has red hair and freckled complexion, (indicating Celticness), and most especially from Liz with her excessively platinum hair. (There is another intriguing dissonance here in that Liz is played by Gia Carides, an actor of Greek origin; her sister, Zoë plays a Greek woman in *Death in Brunswick*. It should be noted as well that Scott is also played by the rather Italio-ethnic-sounding Paul Mercurio.) The effect of this 'ethnicising' of Scott Hasting is to perhaps allow Scott to make the transition into ethnic culture more easy, to make of him a more acceptable transitional character who, in effect, mediates between the two cultures, representing a possibly utopian example of how they might meet and mingle. So that, in the final scene, as Scott and Fran dance together, each is dressed in ethnic—specifically Spanish—style and seem to be, to all intents and purposes, 'the same'; they simultaneously look ethnic and yet have transcended any such narrow definition of ethnicity based in appearance alone.

Ethnic films routinely use a narrowly defined concept of ethnicity, and in so doing reflect the contemporary public discourse of multiculturalism. That is, ethnicity is seen to be a matter of external cultural attributes (physical appearance, dress, language and behaviour), of certain cultural practices (dance, music, cuisine, religion), and of separateness through closed communities which maintain their own traditions and sense of identity drawn from their origins. This is the case with *Strictly Ballroom*, but it does create the ethnicity of its characters and locations with what are quite light (although not necessarily delicate) brushstrokes. Fran's ethnicity, let alone its bearing on the development of the narrative and its resolution, does not become apparent until Scott walks with her to her home, and this takes place both well into the narrative and, through the internal calendar of that narrative, some weeks after they have first begun secretly dancing together. There is a hint, of course, in that very first clandestine dance, when Fran unexpectedly does a few flamenco-type rhythmic heel stamps. Although Scott asks, 'Where did that come from? ', Fran's answer, 'It's a few steps I've been working on at home' is sufficiently vague as to go unnoticed. The importance of Fran's ethnicity does not become apparent, indeed vital for the narrative (and the themes) until Scott confronts her father and his friends at the fiesta at Fran's home. (Having a 'fiesta' at home is a decidedly ethnic thing to do. A similar event begins and ends another Ethnic film, *Looking for Alibrandi* [Kate Woods 2000]) It is here that the film presents then resolves a contradiction and makes clear a theme. The contradiction is that, at first, Fran's cultural milieu seems as restrictive as Scott's. Her father is a demanding patriarch — although his insistence that Fran stay at home is initially ignored. She returns home after being rejected by Shirley Hastings, and sits timorously at the edge of the festivities, not seemingly truly part of them, reflecting the partial movement into Anglo-Australian (ballroom) culture she has made but from which she has been repelled. She tells Scott, who comes looking for her, to 'Go away. I'll get into trouble' by which it can be assumed she will get into trouble from her severe patriarchal father. Yet this is a significant moment in the development of the narrative. Previously Fran has attempted to make the transition from ethnic culture into Anglo-Australian culture but she has only been successful up to the point that Scott has accepted her. The rest of that culture does not accept her. Now Scott will become the one who attempts to bridge the gap from the other direction and enter Fran's culture, not that this is what is on his mind at this particular moment. It is the confrontation with the aggressive patriarch Rico that will bring it about. Beyond whatever psychoanalytical interpretations might be made of Rico's extremely hostile rejection of Scott—I am always delighted by the Freudian possibilities of Rico's demand of Scott: 'Show me your paso doble'—the rejection also seems to be on cultural grounds: Scott is not a member of Rico's ethnic group.

It is by no means clear why Scott claims to dance the paso doble with Fran. This is the first time the name is mentioned; up until now, Scott has been interested in introducing his new steps into the either the samba (as the dance is announced at the Waratah Championships where all the trouble starts) or the rumba, which is mentioned several times and which he and Fran decide is the best one to do at the Pan Pacifics (have they actually been rehearsing other dances as well?). But more importantly, when Scott demonstrates his version of what he calls (or understands to be) a paso doble, his steps are laughed at and dismissed. Dance-wise things get more confusing when Rico demonstrates the 'correct' (i.e., ethnic) way to do these steps—which seem to be flamenco rather than paso doble (raising an unresolved question about whether Fran's family are Spanish or Latin American).[39] Scott's attempts are laughable and dismissed because they are not the way this culture insists they should be done; they do not conform to the rules, only the rules of what?—the traditional folk culture, or South American ballroom dancing? The paso doble is not, it seems, a folk dance; it is a Latin American ballroom dance, curiously, despite its name and that it features a double step, based on the 'one-step' which is a jazz or ragtime ballroom dance created in the United States in the 1920s[40]. Whatever it is that Rico does, he does it by angrily demonstrating the correct steps, to the admiration of those assembled at the fiesta, and then dismisses Fran's efforts as a waste of time. As there is no evidence before (or even after) this to suggest that Rico, let alone Ya Ya, are exponents of ballroom dancing in their own country of origin, the connotation is that they dance from within the folk culture of those origins rather than the ersatz culture of ballroom dancing. This is made more obvious by the complete lack of semblance between what has been shown of ballroom dancing (in the Anglo-Australian context) and that which Rico and Ya Ya perform. Whatever they are doing, they are doing because they are ethnic—which also translates as their knowing better because they are ethnic.

Of greater importance to the film's narrative and themes than whether the dance is flamenco, paso doble or anything else is that this action draws a parallel between Fran's ethnic community and the ballroom community in that neither permit the license to dance outside its particular conventions and rules. Where ethnicity proves superior to Australicity is that a representative of the ethnic culture— Fran's grandmother Ya Ya—steps in to insist that Scott be accepted (as having potential to learn the 'right' way) but, more than this, that paso doble (or flamenco) can be adapted to provide a hybrid of (Australian) ballroom dancing and (ethnic) folk dancing. The ethnic community, seemingly at first rigid and traditional (a common perception in Ethnic films), is revealed to be flexible, 'free', open to outsiders, and fully capable of adjusting to changing situations The theme is introduced and developed from here on: to paraphrase George Orwell—'Old Australia bad, New Australia good'. 'New Australia' in the way I am using it here means multicultural Australia.

Strictly Ballroom presents two cultural milieux, which briefly seem to have inflexibility in common, but which soon become contrasting 'systems' vying for the 'soul' of Scott Hastings. The ethnic community is quickly revealed to be the most attractive one—for Scott and for the putative spectator. The unattractiveness of the ballroom dancing (metaphorically traditional Anglo-Australian) culture is so unrelievedly awful that there really is not choice to be made—the dramatic interest is not *should* Scott rebel against it but just *how* Scott will rebel against it; even the success of his rebellion cannot really be in doubt. This might be Romeo and Juliet but it is (that word again) a feel-good Romeo and Juliet, not a tragic one.

There are only one or two of the other Ethnic films which represent Anglo-Australia as negatively as *Strictly Ballroom*. *Silver City* does so; in fact there is scarcely credible 'human' Anglo-Australian in the whole of that film. Other ethnic films are less acerbic—perhaps because their makers are less willing to bite the hand that feeds them, so to speak. *Strictly Ballroom* sugars its pill by its metaphoric, comic and exaggerated mode of presenting traditional Australians. It is an allegory and not a film of social realism and its fairy-tale form together with its sense of humour moves it away from being seen as satirical. The absence of any sense of the actual Australia existing beyond the confines of the realm of ballroom dancing or even the confines of Fran's home serves to focus attention on the allegorical nature of the Ballroom Dancing Federation as standing for a larger, less obviously cohesive or integrated but nonetheless real Anglo-Australia and Anglo-Australian sense of identity.

Although I have spent time and words on describing the ethnicity of Fran and her family and how this is achieved, that they are ethnic at all does still need some explanation. In the abstract, there is no narrative 'need' for Fran's family to be ethnic. What is important for the story is that a reason is provided for Fran being Juliet to Scott's Romeo. Further, the narrative must provide a source of support, confirmation, and revelation for Scott and Fran's challenge to the rigidity and oppressiveness of the Ballroom Dancing Federation (and all it represents). There is no reason, in purely story-telling terms, why the romantic plot and the dramatic tension and actions produced by the differences between Scott and Fran need to be provided by Fran's situation of an 'outsider' (of being Cinderella, remember,) being caused by her ethnicity. That Fran and her family are ethnic is, however, highly significant in the Australian context; their ethnicity touches upon a raft of social matters lying within the present Australian cultural psyche. The extent to which this is deliberate is unclear. My own feeling is that this is unconscious, but my earlier loose speculation on the ethnic 'nature' of Baz Luhrmann's name should not be entirely dismissed. Film writers and filmmakers often use significant (i.e., signifying) material (ideas, attitudes, perceptions as well as 'actual' conditions and situations) without quite realising why they are using it, let alone fully appreciating its significance. Ethnicity may simply be an obvious way of indicating difference, obviating lengthy explanations through narrative exposition. In the Australian context, to be ethnic can be narrative shorthand for difference. Even so, *Strictly Ballroom* is an Australian film, which celebrates ethnicity to an extent which is not quite as obvious in other Ethnic films, let alone non-ethnic films. It is less clear that it celebrates multiculturalism: although it may be argued that it rightly condemns traditional Anglo-Australian culture, any fully workable notion of multiculturalism must also 'allow' the existence of Anglo-Australian culture as much as it does any ethnic culture. But, of course, *Strictly Ballroom* does not simply present multiculturalism as a good thing, but in fact demonstrates not so much a maintaining of boundaries without barriers (which multiculturalism implies), but a meeting and mingling of cultures—an opening out of both ethnic culture (to allow Scott ingress and for him to merge both ballroom and ethnic dance forms) and of Anglo-Australian culture—the acceptance and acclaim of Scott and Fran's innovatory dancing. Whether it means to be or not, *Strictly Ballroom* is a social critique; by making Cinderella ethnic it says much and implies more about the cultural perception of multiculturalism in Australia. And in so doing, the film has become strangely prophetic. Its representation of 'old' Australia as fearful of the new, of determined to maintain an outmoded set of rules, of being determined to resist change, all of which looked (or could be overlooked as) quaint and humorous, as an amusing set of references to certain archaic Australian attitudes, took on new meaning with political events in Australia a few years later and continues to resonate through the official policies related to 'boat people' and 'detainees'. This feel-good film became, in retrospect a film that in fact had an unexpected 'message' about fear lurking at the communal heart of Australia.

Half-lives and Half-lies

Practically all feature films tell stories. All such stories, in order to be understood (and to be more than just a 'summary') take a particular form usually called narratives. That is, they are structured in their telling. And a key element in that structure is the disruption, or an event, an incident, something that happens to cause the narrative to develop (and work towards a resolution). Put simply, to ask why a certain action or event causes a disruption (and so causes the whole narrative in fact) is to ask quite a large question about a film.

The disruption that sets the narrative going in *Strictly Ballroom* is the moment when Scott dances his own steps at the Waratah Championships. Unlike many narratives which start with some sense of an equilibrium to set the time, place and characters into a status quo, *Strictly Ballroom* begins with the disruption. In fact, it really begins with reactions to the disruption through the pseudo-documentary interviews intercut with footage of the championships. These interviews reinforce the disruption by, if anything, over-emphasising the extraordinary nature of the event. This overemphasis is, of course, necessary for the dramatic developments (the consequences and complications) that will follow. What is not clear is just why Scott dancing his own steps should be a problem; that it is a very real problem is demonstrated by the manner in which the incident echoes and re-echoes, is discussed and re-discussed for a considerable amount of narrative time (during which the equilibrium is also being sketched in, giving the perspective against which the disruption and, more importantly, its consequences will be measured). The true nature of the problems caused by Scott dancing his own steps, and the consequence of his refusing to 'recant', do not become available immediately. Why shouldn't he be allowed to dance his own steps? This is not clear; what is clear is that he should not, and that he will be expected to submit and not persist in wanting to do so (expected by others in the story, not the spectators who, one might reasonably assume, are sufficiently aware of narratives to know or hope that he won't). The immediate consequences are broadly two-fold: Scott wants to go on dancing his own steps; others—Les, Barry, Shirley—want him to desist. Fran's 'arrival' is an unexpected complication (another aspect of narrative structure) but, for purposes of pursuing the narrative and, especially, for resolving it a vital one.

So much so that, in narrative structural terms, it might seem that a second disruption occurs when Fran, rejected by Scott, accuses him of being 'gutless'. If one postulates a new status quo (a new equilibrium) in which Scott dances his own steps for and by himself (the theme of narcissism again), then Fran's interruption is both a literal and a narrative disruption. Fran's approach to Scott is crucial for the narrative, but what is crucial for the theme of the film is her claim that he is 'really scared'. In so doing she touches upon something hidden deep in Scott's subconscious. He cannot, or does not, respond directly to the accusation or even to the vehemence with which it is uttered but nonetheless it is this accusation which causes his abrupt about-face. He almost immediately regrets this decision when she cannot even manage the basic opening steps.[41]

The truth of Fran's charge of fear preventing action or initiative takes a long time to become apparent to Scott, to percolate up from his subconscious. But it does so later when he blurts out to Shirley, Les and others—almost as if discovering it himself for the first time—'You're all so scared, you wouldn't know what you wanted'. Ironically, these allegations are not openly demonstrated to be true— although some of the characters show symptoms. At the time of Fran accusing Scott of being gutless, there is little which has been seen or heard that would support the charge. If anything, Scott seems quite courageous (in a personal-psychological way) for wanting to persevere with his own steps—even if he is doing so late at night when he thinks he is alone, unobserved and unlikely to be restrained by Les (as he has been earlier when Les 'partners' him while remonstrating with him).

The accusation that will echo: "vivir com miedo, es comovivir a medias'.

Fran's earlier charge is even more unexpected than Scott's reiteration of it—and thus underlines the importance of this theme of fear—because the film apparently intends its putative audience to assume that her interest in Scott is purely sexual. In this the film offers no explanation for Fran spying on Scott, at least no 'stated' explanation—Fran's claim to make up her own steps seems largely irrelevant (although a couple of steps she does at one point do impress

Scott). Scott, at this moment, is at his most sexually attractive, Fran at her least attractive. It is 'obvious' therefore why she would firstly watch Scott and secondly approach him, and her flustered, confused attempts at conversation underline this implication of sexual interest. Thus, the charge of Scott being afraid comes as a surprise. It is not simply the spiteful retort of a young woman whose advances (made with great difficulty, even great courage) have been rejected, although it is to some extent that. It is the precise nature of the charge: that Scott is 'gutless'; not that he is too vain, too proud, too arrogant or even too self-absorbed to want to dance with a 'beginner' and a rather plain one at that. Fran's elaboration that 'you're really scared to give someone new a go because you think, you know, they might just be better than you are' is equally baseless in terms of any evidence the film has provided to this point. There is something ironic about it given what will be revealed later of Fran's situation as 'new' in terms of being a beginner in ballroom dancing and in terms of her family being 'new' Australians. But it sounds, and presumably is intended to sound, like the retort of someone rejected and emotionally lashing out.

The terms of the charge are so unexpected, and so unsupported by the narrative to that point that the importance of it to the narrative and for the thematic of the film are heavily underlined. (This is one of the moments, common in narrative films, where the film 'tells' what is on its mind.) This emphasis is, however, simultaneously confirmed and diminished by Scott's change of heart. That he does decide to dance with Fran indicates the bolt has found its mark. That he does not explain why he is doing so (e.g., saying something along the lines of 'I'll show you whether I am gutless or not') or even attempt to meet the charge '(e.g., 'I'm not afraid') allows the narrative importance of the fear theme to remain understated but crucially not unstated. It may possibly be interpreted that it is Fran's bursting into tears after this outburst that changes Scott's mind. Nonetheless, fear is quite obviously something the film 'has on its mind'. Within the outburst by Fran, the word 'scared' is used twice, as is the word 'gutless', and it is concluded by what will become both an epigram and a motif for the film 'vivir con miedo, es como virir a medias' which is later translated by Fran as 'To live with fear is a life half lived'.

Later the situation has shifted, or the scales have fallen from Scott's eyes. It is when he is being bulldozed into dancing with Tina Sparkle, that he accuses Shirley, Les Kendall and others of 'all being so scared, you wouldn't know what you thought'. Again this is something of an accusation coming out of left field. It is not by any means clear of what Shirley, Les and the others might be scared (although Barry Fife's ominous and bullying character has made itself slightly apparent by this time). The motivation for Shirley and Les would seem to be to produce a winning dancer; they seem driven by a desire to win rather than by fear. This will prove to be a narrative red herring, however. All the same, this does not seem to be what Scott is implying. It could be thought that Scott's charge is related to nobody being willing or able to tell Scott what is wrong with the way he dances. He has directed this very question at them at this very point. In retrospect, this is a trifle odd as Les Kendall has quite early on has explained it: lack of 'floor craft', 'no energy driven into the floor', 'untidy hands and feet', 'you could have driven a truck between your left elbow and right hand' and so on. This moment of accusation stands as a reiteration of the first, important but as yet unsupported. It emphasises, however, that the official 'explanation' of why he must not dance his own steps and/or with Fran is not acceptable to Scott, that something lies behind it, that it is a cover for something that cannot be openly admitted or acknowledged. Thus his accusation that they are all scared ensures that the theme remains present and acknowledged even if it still has not been explained. If it isn't the way Scott dances that has them all scared, then it is that he dances or threatens to dance differently that has them scared. This then indicates one of the specific fears that shape and inform the film's themes: the fear of nonconformity.

To come to grips with this theme of fear, it is worth tracing the progress of the expression Fran uses: 'Vivir con miedo, es como virir a medias'. Its first utterance is actually also the first hint that Fran is or may be ethnic. But it seems to be inexplicable—to non-Spanish speakers—and there is no subtitle translation unlike the later occasional bits of dialogue in Spanish. Indeed, to an untutored ear there is probably nothing which would cause it to be identified as Spanish. The fact that it is Spanish seems to have no immediate implications. It is, seemingly, an insult of some sort spoken in a foreign language. That it is even an insult or an expression of anger can only be gauged from the context of Fran's passionate response to Scott's rejection of her overture. That whatever it means may have some connection with fear can only be inferred in that it follows hard upon Fran's accusation of gutlessness. It is almost immediately put to one side; Scott does not ask, 'What did you say?' or 'What does that mean?'. The film is saving that for later. Fran bursts into tears; Scott asks her name.

The term is then forgotten for a long period. In terms of story time within the narrative, it is at least several weeks — Shirley Hastings's hands crossing days off a calendar ensure a sense of this. The term reappears as Scott walks Fran home after they have been practising in secret throughout this period, although this is possibly the first time he walks her home since he seems a bit uncertain of where they are. He is trying out the expression, which, when he manages to say it correctly, Fran translates as 'to live with fear is a life half lived'. Scott repeats, 'a life half lived', and claims to like the expression. There is no reason why he should 'like' it. As a proverb, let alone as a statement of a philosophy, there is nothing about what is known of Scott at this point to suggest a reason for the idea contained within the expression to appeal to him. It does have a mellifluous ring to it, in English or in Spanish, but he seems to appreciate the sentiment rather than the sound. Narratively, it is important that it is emphasised that Scott 'likes it' because this very notion of living a life in fear will be said at the climactic point when Scott is about to betray Fran and himself and all they have worked for. It will be the trigger than ensures the last minute arrival of the appropriate resolution to the drama. It is important, then, that Scott both find out what it means (and in so doing, of course, lets the audience in on the secret) and to reveal a concern with the notion that a life can be half lived if fear is allowed to control one's destiny. The scene is important too because through it the saying will become something else that Scott and Fran share; it will become a sort of talisman for them.

Starling news: 'You're all so scared'.

Having been initially raised in a subtle fashion, then explained and given increasing if as yet unclear narrative significance, the phrase once more drops out of sight (or perhaps more accurately, out of hearing). But in leit-motif fashion, it returns at another key moment of tension between Scott and Fran. This is, in keeping with the mirror-image theme in *Strictly Ballroom*, a 'mirror image' of the first time. Now, however, Scott has pursued Fran, after she has fled or been driven away from the ballroom by Shirley. Fran's original words, 'I want to dance with you' are repeated by Scott to explain why he is there and what he wants with her and when she tells him to go away (a reversal of his rejection of her), he uses her line, in English this time, against her when he charges her with, 'What happened to a life lived in fear and all that stuff?'. Fran does not answer the charge directly, as Scott did not the first time, but the fear of being different (part of the fear of nonconformity) is clearly on her mind. Scott is now prepared to ignore this fear, and to embrace difference—'I don't want you to be like them'—and further is more 'afraid' of losing Fran than of losing the dance competition through not conforming—'I just want to dance our steps'. He at least has moved beyond fear (if he ever felt it), driven now by a growing emotional attachment to Fran rather than himself and his dancing. His lack of fear manifests itself further in his confrontation with Fran's father that follows. (Scott's backing away and falling over a pile of trash is caution rather than fear.)

The film is not ready to relinquish this useful reminder of what it is 'about' quite yet; it has further service to do in helping drive and resolve the narrative. If Scott has embraced the philosophic ideal it encapsulates, Fran, ironically, has not. It would seem knowing the phrase and acting by its precept are two different things. She has to be reminded of it by Ya Ya as they prepare a dress for Fran to wear at the forthcoming Pan Pacific Championships. Fran is still afraid of being different, concerned that people will laugh at her—presumably as a result of the reaction of Shirley and Liz at the State Championships although she was ready to dance in public with Scott there. Her concern that people will laugh at her seems to be because she feels that she is unattractive rather than that she will be wearing an authentic (ethnic) dress, different from the gaudy kitsch of the ballroom dance fraternity. Ya Ya reminds her of 'vivir con miedo...', assuring her that to be beautiful all she has to do is 'not be scared'. Scott's wholesale embracing of the saying and what it means as a rule to live by is not so readily followed by Fran. Perhaps as an Anglo-Australian and a male, he has less to be scared of. As a thoroughgoing outsider, Fran has more to be frightened of in venturing into the world of ballroom dancing with the express purpose of flouting its rules and conventions. It may be that she is more capable of assessing the consequences of her actions than the less introspective Scott.

The film is not yet finished with repetitions and references to this phrase. When Scott and Fran are ready to tackle the championships with their new dance style, arrived at through the tutelage of Rico, Scott is simultaneously ready to recognise his attraction to Fran. Fran has of course been in love with Scott from the outset. In recognising this and consummating it—with a kiss, this is a fairy tale still—Scott uses the term light-heartedly, as if it were a shared joke between them, almost as it they recognise that it was what brought them together in the first place, and that it no longer applies to them. In the dramatic sense, it is also an ironical repetition because they are the last words Scott says to Fran before 'betraying' her as a result of Barry Fife's mendacious revelations of Doug Hastings' past. However, it would be going too far to suggest that Scott's motivation in deciding to dance with his previous partner Liz and to 'dump' Fran is one of fear as such. There is a further irony in the fact that Scott's newly discovered capacity to move beyond self-love to be able to love and express love for another should be manipulated by Barry Fife in a way that forces Scott to put the well-being of his father (whom he has previously largely ignored) before his own (and Fran's). A convenient narrative ellipsis avoids revealing how the decision not to dance with her was conveyed to Fran, let alone why Scott didn't also explain it at the same time. For the sake of a satisfyingly dramatic climax and resolution, it is necessary that Fran does not know.

That Fran doesn't know (or the plot does not show her being told by Scott or anyone else) yet is somehow (if inexplicably) aware that she is 'back in beginners where she belongs' and so turns up at the Pan Pacific Championships actually dancing in the beginners' section enables another dramatic confrontation and the opportunity for Fran to reverse the cycle, so to speak, and throw Scott's very words back at him. When he catches up with her, she now takes his words to her and demands, 'What happened to a life lived in fear and all that stuff', and goes back to their first meeting by reiterating, 'You really are a gutless wonder.' Of course, it is known (by the audience but not by Fran because of the use of this ellipsis) that Scott is not acting out of fear. The false accusation is doubly unfair because Scott is motivated by a concern for another other than himself, something he has learnt how to do because of Fran's love for him.

The phrase, or a literal echo of it, makes its final appearance (for the dramatic and narrative effect all these repetitions and reminders have been intended to have all along) at the very point of climax. The climax, like all 'good' narrative climaxes, occurs at that point when the narrative cannot bear any more consequences and complications; the dramatic tension must be released, the resolution must take place, and it all must do so in keeping with the direction the narrative has been heading since the outset. Scott is about to complete his betrayal of Fran, and demolish any hope for change, change which, while feared by nearly everyone, is clearly what the narrative has directed the audience to want have happen (and which in the way this narrative is organised, must happen). With Scott's imminent return to the fold, Barry Fife looks set to win; the full extent of his villainy is disclosed by the intercutting of scenes of his corrupt fixing of the contest with scenes of Doug Hastings' denial of the story Fife has told Scott. Doug finally gets Scott to listen to him, when he reveals that Barry has lied twice — once in the past to prevent Doug from dancing his own steps and again to prevent Scott from dancing his.

Ironically, Doug's insistence on speaking with Scott prevents Scott from being able to explain to Fran, but this is simply to heighten the dramatic tension of the moment.

'We lived our lives in fear.'

Fear raises its head not only in the true history of Doug and Shirley's past but in the way in Shirley still wants Scott to dance Federation steps with Liz. She is afraid of the insecurity—economic insecurity—that going against the Federation would have brought and can still bring. It is now revealed that this is the same fear that motivated her in the past to dance with Les and not Doug, to dance Federation and not Doug's own steps. Even now, Shirley's influence over Scott, seen throughout the narrative and implied from the outset, is more powerful than Doug, who has been portrayed as ineffectual and in Shirley's shadow throughout. Scott is about to go onto the floor and dance with Liz, capitulation is near, but Doug's final words to Scott are 'we've lived our lives in fear', and the 'fear' echoes on the soundtrack, in Scott's head, around the ballroom. Each preceding reiteration of the motif now receives its narrative justification. The effect is to cause Scott to abandon Liz and, yet again, to pursue Fran. Now facing not only their fears but also the fears of Shirley and Doug, Scott and Fran face Barry Fife. The act of courage is supported by others and Barry Fife is defeated.

A question may be asked of this film and indeed any film: why this resolution? But this question is seldom asked of narrative feature films because of the way in which the narrative has been constructed, has worked towards a 'natural' resolution, a resolution that has been prepared for by ensuring it is the 'correct' one, the one the audience has been directed to expect, even to want. Thus, in the case of *Strictly Ballroom*, it would be ludicrous to resolve the situation by, say, Scott simply turning his back on all these lies and fears and restrictions, and disappearing into the sunset with (or without) Fran. This is, of course, simply kite-flying. My point is just to emphasise through the use of a hypothetical 'alternative' that the resolution must solve the problem of ballroom dancing being an oppressive and unhealthy regime while, at the same time, meeting the requirements of Scott and Fran 'fulfilling their destiny'. The problem is not simply that they, narratively, must live happily ever afterwards but the manner in which they do so. Their disrupted and threatened relationship can only be restored by the destruction of the tyranny of Barry Fife (or what that tyranny represents). The point then is that while this resolution seems to be the only one that makes sense, is 'naturalised' in that sense, it is also open to examination in order to see just what it is offering. In this case, rather transparently, it is offering the throwing off of fear and the consequential collapse of the source of and the reasons for that fear. A number of clichés suggest themselves to encapsulate the meaning of this resolution: 'we have nothing to fear but fear itself'; or 'to thine ownself be true'.

And, of course, the film has provided all along what the solution is: don't live in fear, or you will only half live. To parody Shakespeare then, the theme of *Strictly Ballroom* might be summed up as 'To be afraid or not to be afraid, that is the question'. The answer is, of course, not to be afraid. And, finally, no one is. And particularly, no one is any longer afraid of change. So the resolution does not simply say, face your fears (to continue the Shakespearean paraphrase) and on a dance floor of troubles oppose and end them; but oppose and end them in the name of change and for the purpose of embracing change, difference and the refusal to conform.

Strictly Ballroom is not only about fear, it is also crucially about the triumphing over fear, about the rejection of a life half-lived. The idea of a life half-lived is not simply a personal credo, it is a social imperative as well. In terms of *Strictly Ballroom* as a metaphor for contemporary Australia, the fears it elucidates are particularly potent. The fear of difference is linked with two other fears: fear of outsiders, and fear of change. These two fears are, within the film, part of the same thing. The fear of change is the more obvious, the more overt fear; fear of outsiders is less clearly expressed in the narrative but implicit in the way in which Fran, the catalyst of change, is an outsider. I have already discussed the over-determination of Fran's outsider status by making her ethnic. Nonetheless, the film makes sure that her outsider status is understood not only implicitly by making her come from a clearly foreign or alien background and home circumstances but explicitly from her own mouth. As the narrative reaches its climax, as Fran turns on Scott, convinced he has betrayed her because when the crunch comes he is afraid of change or of being different (which can only work dramatically not logically as he has never shown this to be the case, even when accused of it at the very beginning—Fran is wrong both times), she refers explicitly to the manner in which her difference has been thrown in her face. In the Cinderella speech, she not only refers to the way she has been made to do menial tasks around Kendall's dance studio, presumably because of her status as an outsider anxious to be allowed in to the 'hallowed' circle of ballroom dancing, but also of the cruel jibes about her name, 'Frangipanidelasqueeegymop'. This nickname has both the elements of the Cinderella construction—the reference to 'squeegee mop' being like the reference to cinders, a denotation of her role—and also, presumably to her ethnic family name. This last is never given, in the film or even in the script, but it is probably Dela-something or other than sounds like 'squeegee'.

This said, it must be registered that the film does not, for the most part, make clear that the objections of others to Fran are based on her being ethnic, and up until she is seen dancing backstage with Scott, they are not afraid of her or what she potentially represents. In fact, other than for one use by Liz of the nickname, Frangipanni, and Shirley's patronising comments on her complexion, there is very little to suggest that characters within the narrative dislike Fran at all until that moment. Liz is, after all, just a self-seeking bitch and, if the accusation of being afraid of giving someone new a go because they might be better than you are is true of anyone, it is true of Liz. The fear of difference is registered as a subtext to the metaphoric presentation of ballroom dancing as traditional Anglo-Australia. If, using this interpretation, Anglo-Australia is afraid of change, then it is afraid of the change that 'aliens in our midst' threaten to bring about. Without Fran and without the ethnicity, the difference provided by her family, Scott's attempts to go against the rules of the Federation would have come to nothing. The film certainly falls a long way short of having Barry Fife scapegoat Fran—he is almost oblivious to her existence and can only refer to her as 'and partner' when he tries to get Scott and Fran off the dance floor. If anything, it is Scott's fault for dancing with Fran in the first instance and then mixing with and learning from her culture. Thus the scapegoating of 'non-Australians' which was attempted (or perhaps revived) a few years later in the political arena in Australia has no direct counterpart in the film. The social reference, or social prophecy, is to the rigidity of traditional Australia and its refusal to permit change. *Strictly Ballroom* is thoroughly in favour of multiculturalism but the unconsciousness of its exploration of this is demonstrated by the way in which Fife and others do not use this as grounds for objecting to Fran or even to what Scott is doing. Ethnicity is selected as an obvious indicator of difference and multiculturalism as cause for hope, but the film does not consciously offer this as a thesis to be explored.

Who then is afraid in *Strictly Ballroom*? I have argued that, despite Fran's twice repeated charges, Scott is not. I think this is demonstrably so. I have also argued that on a number of occasions, Fran is. But equally, she faces her fears especially at the very beginning when she approaches Scott. Others demonstrate behaviours which might be considered fearful, to reveal lurking terrors, psychologically speaking. Liz and Shirley are two obvious candidates for this. Both function at levels of or just below hysteria. Liz wails 'like a banshee'[42] both times when Scott 'abandons' her.

She is afraid of change and nonconformity, utterly unable to cope with the idea of being Scott's partner in new steps. Shirley gives less spectacular vent to her repressed

Banshee-wailer extraordinaire Liz:- disappointment and
tantrums her fear-driven lot.

hysteria but it is present just below the surface in the sequence in Kendall's dance studio after the 'débacle' at the Waratah Championships, before revealing itself when she bursts into tears there and later at home contemplating Scott's intransigence and again when she slaps Scott's face after he tells her he does not care about winning. But it is most obvious at the climax, when Doug reveals the truth, and Shirley attempts to deny it. Shirley, through Doug, reveals her deep-seated fear of being different, which would in her mind have had severe consequences on their futures.

Fear of change is what motivates Barry Fife's actions throughout. He is given a moment of apparent justification when he tells Les Kendall that he 'loves dancing' and is not willing to 'let what we have fought for all these years to be destroyed'. Whether he does love dancing is far from clear; he may just be conning Les, again. Of course, the idea that they have 'fought for' dancing is highly reminiscent of 'traditional' Anglo-Australians claiming they too have fought for Australia (literally in a couple of wars) and are not prepared to see it destroyed—by changes they don't approve of. For the most part Fife is simply fighting against change because he fears it, and his fear is to a large extent justified; change will destroy him or at least topple him from his position of power. The film makes it quite clear that this is what he deserves and that it is a fitting manner in which change can be brought about and celebrated. Fear of change is shown to be groundless except for those who have a vested interest in maintaining the status quo. Shirley and even perhaps Liz think they have such an interest, but as the proverb so neatly encapsulates, the status quo only provides them with a half-life and a fearful one at that.

There can be little doubt that Shirley and Doug Hastings are the epitome of lives half lived. Throughout, Doug has seemed little more than a cipher—the physical embodiment of someone half alive, even down to his consistent nervous habit of spraying breath freshener into his mouth, a sign perhaps of a psychological sense of decay. He is henpecked by Shirley, and often abused as a silly or stupid man, frequently at points at which Shirley's repressed hysteria is about to erupt. Doug's life of fear is manifest in his very appearance; he looks more than timid, he looks afraid most of the time. He dances his 'manic shuffling' in secret and keeps his mementoes and memories hidden away under lock and key, bringing them out in private and weeping over them. He is totally unable to stand up to the enigmatic charge directed at him (via the way in which Barry and others, including Shirley, look at him) that Scott needs to learn some home truths about where wanting to dance one's own steps can lead. Doug slinks away and presumably does nothing to try and prevent Barry from carrying out this threat. Doug's place as a timid, hen-pecked nonentity, who seems to have little connection to ballroom dancing save through Shirley and Scott's involvement, is important for the force of the revelations and the drama of the climax. He is actually an unintentional object lesson in why, in a way, it is right to be afraid of change and non-conformity: his attempts to change the system have resulted in him living a half-life. But then Doug only had Shirley to rely upon, and Shirley was of the same 'insider-group' as he and she betrayed him in just the way in which Scott is about to do to Fran. Scott is fortunate in that his partner comes from the outside and thus brings the outside with her. Even so, it requires Doug's crucial intervention, his throwing off of his fears, to bring about irrevocable change, and change for the better. Moreover, it is Doug, as much as Scott who recognises Fran's potential as the catalyst that will cause the change. When others dismiss her as irrelevant, it is Doug who ignores them and films Fran dancing in the beginners' at the Pan Pacifics, an action that is crucial in reinforcing the theme and in leading to the climactic revelations. Doug seems drawn to her difference and her courage. Overall, there is a hierarchy of fear, so to speak. Scott is the least afraid; in fact he never acts from fear throughout. Fran is occasionally afraid but also shown to be capable of facing her fear. Doug is the most afraid. It is he who has truly lived a life in fear, a half-life. His facing and denouncing his fear is thus, dramatically, the most significant.

Change is on the agenda in *Strictly Ballroom* and change is what is achieved. Scott Hastings changes from a self-absorbed narcissus to an emotionally mature lover, a champion of and for the people and not simply for himself. Fran changes from a demure and dowdy Cinderella to a beautiful and appropriate princess for Scott's Prince Charming. Doug Hastings casts off his fears and takes his rightful place as Shirley's partner. Ballroom dancing is changed from a closed and ordered world of oppression and fear to a world of openness and joy. The 'lesson' for contemporary Australian within the fairy-tale mode of *Strictly Ballroom* has proved to be a prescient, vital and imaginative one but it is not clear, to me at least, that despite the film's popularity, it is a lesson that has been understood.

NOTES

1. David Stratton. *The Last New Wave*. (Angus and Robertson, Sydney, 1980). My reference to being premature refers to both the stop-and-go nature of film production in Australia since 1970, which has created a sense of there being a series, arguably three at least, of Australian 'new waves', and to the fact that a number of national cinemas have emerged (or re-emerged) globally since, each of which might be considered to be a 'new wave'. The term is perhaps becoming exhausted through being overworked since the original French *nouvelle vague* of the 1950s.
2. The concessions were not entirely removed. Rather, from (at their peak) the ability to write-off 150% of an investment in a feature film, and to only pay tax on 50% of any profit, the 'normal' tax deductions on business investment now apply to film production.
3. The most encyclopaedic source of information on feature films made in Australia since 1977 is Scott Murray (ed), *Australian Feature Films 1978-1994* (Oxford University Press, Melbourne, 1995). The indispensable guide for all Australian films prior to 1977 is Andrew Pike and Cooper, *Australian Film 1900-1977* (Oxford University Press/AFI, Melbourne, 1980).
4. Neil Rattigan, *Images of Australia: 100 Films of the New Australian Cinema* (Southern Methodist University Press, Dallas 1991).
5. A detailed discussion of the post-production marketing and distribution of *Strictly Ballroom* can be found in Mary Anne Reid, *Long Shots to Favourites:*

Australian Cinema Successes in the 90s (Australian Film Commission, Sydney, 1993).

6. Mise-en-scène means 'all the elements placed in front of the camera to be photographed' (David Bordwell and Kristin Thompson, *Film Art: An Introduction*, 7th edition, McGraw Hill, Boston, 2004). Originally a French term, it is variously used in English with and without the accent, equally as uncertainly italicized. I will retain the accent but not the italics—Bordwell and Thompson do not do either.

7. I am speaking here of the post-1970 Australian cinema. The total number of Australian Musical Comedies is not greatly expanded if pre-1970 films are included but it should be recognised there were some made in the 1930s.

8. David Buchbinder, 'Strictly ballsroom', *Performance Anxieties: Re-producing Maculinity* (Sydney, Allen and Unwin, 1998), pp. 48-69.

9. Buchbinder, p.54.

10. If it is accepted that *Proof* is a 'quirky comedy', then it must be credited with preceding even *Strictly Ballroom*. Quirky as *Proof* may be, at best it may be described as a black comedy. It is certainly hard to make a case for it having the 'feel-good' factor that is present in abundance in the 'big three'. *Death in Brunswick* is a more convincing candidate for a pre-*Strictly* quirky comedy.

11. Steven Swann Jones, in *The Fairy Tale: The Magic Mirror of the Imagination* (Twayne, New York, 1995), argues for a "subgenre [of fairy tales] of innocent persecuted heroines [in which the heroine] is persecuted in her parents' home, persecuted in her

attempt to be married and finally persecuted in her husband's home" (p.67) By substituting 'to dance with' for 'to be married' and take 'her husband's home' for the ballroom dancing community of *Strictly Ballroom*, a valid comparison seems supportable.

12. Jones, p.9.

13. Jones, p.11. My emphasis.

14. This capacity of cinema to create a fantastic mise-en-scène which nonetheless benefits by film's aesthetic attraction to verisimilitude is by no means restricted to fairy tales. Indeed, its most prolific use is in two other popular genres: Horror films and Science Fiction.

15. There are also other reasons for Scott's restrained appearance when compared with the flashy *kitsch* of the others. These are connected with characteristics and sexuality, although in the latter regard the avoidance of intimations of 'camp' through Scott's black-and-white restrained ensemble may well be contradicted by, as Buchbinder puts it, '. . . the singleted, hairless or lightly haired muscular torso [being] an icon of the male body desirable to gay men' (p. 59).

16. Buchbinder (p.62-5) argues that the film retains the over-riding patriarchal authority—merely replaying 'bad' patriarch Fife with good 'patriarch' Rico. I do not entirely disagree but the return of the (repressed/usurped) patriarch Doug complicates this simple dichotomy.

17. Jones, p.47.

18. While it may be argues that Rico represents another father for Scott, in fairy-tale terms I see him as a

'supernatural helper' rather than a surrogate father. The two can become fused in modern fairy tales such as the early *Star Wars* films and the Obi Wan Kenobi/Annakin Skywalker/Luke Skywalker relationships.

19. These medieval romances are not fairy tales, presumably, because they are of literary origin and form, and in any case are much too long and narratively elaborate. To me, however, the difference is confusing as the Gail Quest narratives seem to apply the essential criterion of fairy tales through 'the incorporation of magic or fantasy in such a manner that its epistemological and ontological validity is confirmed' and they include (or demand) 'the incorporation of a quest, adventure, or problem, which entails interaction with the unknown or magical realm'. Jones, p.21.

20. As described in the published script of *Strictly Ballroom* (Currency Press, Sydney, 1992) p.32.

21. Jones, p. 17.

22. Marina Warner, *From the Beast to the Blonde: On Fairy Tales and Their Tellers* (The Noonday Press, New York, 1996) p.218.

23. Warner, p.219.

24. Warner, p.219.

25. Warner, p.202.

26. Warner, p.210.

27. W.R.S.Ralston, "Cinderella", reproduced in Alan Dundas, ed, *Cinderella: A Folklore Casebook* (Garland, New York, 1982) pp 32-33.

28. Arthur S. Reber, *The Penguin Dictionary of Psychology* (Penguin, Hardmondsworth, 1985).

29. The published script of *Strictly Ballroom* confirms what is obvious visually on the screen when it describes Scott's dance as 'this dance of dark and passionate beauty' (p.22). The extent to which this published script is constructed from the finished film rather than the original screenplay is unclear. That is, are these words an attempt to describe what happens in and by the film or did the original script call for a 'dance of dark and passionate beauty'?

30. As I have introduced psycho-analysis into this discussion, I should point out that at least one influential theory of narcissism holds that it is caused by a lack of care and attention to the infant by its mother. Refer to Andrew M. Colman, ed. *Companion Encyclopaedia to Psychology*, Vol. 2. (Routledge, London and New York), pp.1268-69.

31. It is interesting to note that the published script resorts to a fairy-tale reference to describe what happens at this moment: "Like the child seeing the emperor's new clothes, he realises there is nothing there" (when looking at Tina Sparkle and her partner (p.41).

32. Jack Zipes, *Fairy Tales as Myth, Myth as Fairy Tale*, (University of Kentucky, Lexington, 1994) p.33.

33. Buchbinder; John Champagne 'Dancing Queen: Feminist and Gay Male Spectatorship in Three Recent Films from Australia', *Film Criticism*, vol.21, no.3, Spring 1977, pp.66-88.

34. Zipes (1994), p.37.

35. This is not a universally held position amongst folklorists. Jack Zipes, for example, assets that 'Insofar as [fairy tales] have tended to project other and better worlds, they have often been considered

subversive...'. Jack Zipes, *Breaking the Magic Spell: Radical Theories of Folk and Fairy Tales* (Heinemann, London, 1979) p.3.

36.   A term first used, as far as I can tell, by Susan Dermody and Elizabetha Jacka in *The Screening of Australia, Volume 2: Anatomy of an Industry* (Currency Press, Sydney, 1988): 'The most obvious aesthetic grouping among the films since 1970 is the picturesque period film formed in the wake of the success in 1975 of *Picnic at Hanging Rock*' (p.31).

37.   *Priscilla* does make a cheap jibe at the expense of a Filipino mail-order bride but this hardly constitutes an examination of ethnicity in contemporary Australia.

38.   Spanish-speaking ethnicity is unusual in Australian film and perhaps in Australian society. Within the Ethnic film genre, this is the only such film; the greater percentage are about Greek ethnicity with Italian ethnicity a close second.

39.   The uncertainty about flamenco or paso doble is passingly raised in the published script when the first time Fran does some steps when rehearsing with Scott, she 'explodes into a flurry of flamenco steps' (p.24). At no time does it later describe anything Rico does or teaches them to do as anything but paso doble. It does, however, describe the dress Fran is having altered for the championships as 'Ya Ya's flamenco dress' (p.54).

40.   Or (according to the Australian Broadcasting Commission in a definition provided on the Internet to support a ballroom dancing program it produced in 2005), 'Synonymous with Spanish culture, the Paso Doble is a traditional folk dance, that is more

commonly performed as a competition or exhibition dance, rather than a social dance. The name "Paso Doble" in Spanish means "two step". The "two step" refers to the marching nature of the steps, and the dance is recognisable by its dramatic poses that usually mirror highlights in the music'. Other sources place its origins in France. The term seems flexible enough to be applied at different times to different dance activities. There *are* moments in Scott's performance which do support connections with a bullfight march—not that Rico is ever shown teaching Scott *these* steps.

41.　Fran says something odd at this point: 'You said an hour'. Scott said nothing of the sort. This suggests something of this scene has ended up on the cutting room floor. Much the same thing happens when Ya Ya first approaches Scott after his ludicrous demonstration in front of Fran's father. Fran, appearing to translate, says to Scott, 'Grandma would like to teach us'. Grandma has not said this (at least according to the translation via the subtitles), although perhaps it is the implication of her remarks.

42.　Script, p.15.

STRICTLY BALLROOM — SELECTED CREDITS.

Director:	Baz Luhrmann
Writers:	Baz Luhrmann and Craig Pearce
Producers:	Tristram Miall (producer), Antoinette Albert (executive producer), Jane Scott (line producer)
Cinematography:	Steve Mason
Editing:	Jill Bilcock
Production Design:	Catherine Martin
Art Direction:	Martin Brown
Original music:	David Hirschfelder
Costume design:	Angus Stathie

Principal Cast

Paul Mercurio	Scott Hastings
Tara Morice	Fran
Bill Hunter	Barry Fife
Pat Thompson	Shirley Hastings
Gia Carides	Liz Holt
Peter Whitford	Les Kendall
Barry Otto	Doug Hastings
John Hannah	Ken Railings
Sonia Kruger	Tina Sparkle

Kris McQuade	Charm Leachman
Pip Mushin	Wayne Burns
Antonio Vargas	Rico
Armonia Benedito	Ya Ya
Jack Webster	Terry
Lauren Hewett	Kylie Hastings
Steve Grace	Luke
Paul Bertram	MC